THE TAINTED VIEW

WRITTEN BY

KRISTINA LANDERS

ISBN: 0-75961-816-X

This book is printed on acid free paper.

1stBooks - rev. 02/24/01

INTRODUCTION

I have concocted this book despite the negative feedback that may surface in time. When you read my theories about life, please try to be open-minded. Realize that it is just one person's over-opinionated outlook; the world through the eyes of a young adult. I would also like this book to act as an outlet for people who don't have the opportunity, or maybe even the courage to speak their mind. This is not a self-help escape to some ridiculous miracle, it is simply words on paper to be translated any way you deem appropriate. I don't wish to influence or persuade anyone's viewpoint to suit my convictions. I am not a pessimist, nor do I choose to wither in self-pity over the injustices of life. Therefore, I share my feelings without caution, as we so often neglect to do in our everyday lives.

Let me start by telling you a little bit about myself. My name is Kristina Landers, and I am a 25-year-old assistant manager in a well established video store. I have attended college, however, I have not obtained a college degree. I have also studied many other alternative schooling courses, and thus far I am still sitting in a job where I am overwhelmed with feeling of under-accomplishment. Someday I will be free from the chains of the corporate gurus, but until then I am where I am.

I am also a vegetarian and a supporter in the animal rights movement. I volunteer my time to wildlife rehabilitation, and I have played an active role in raising orphaned animals until they are able to fend for themselves in a natural environment.

At this point I will not continue to bore you with the details of my life, although the subject may be sparked at a later time. I am merely opening the door for you to poke fun at my life as I will be at many of your ideas. Keep in mind that ridicule is not the sole controversy that dictates every chapter, but be forewarned it most definitely ties into the appropriate subjects. As I stated before, this is not my way of unleashing anyone's demon. It is merely a few thoughts coupled with an opinion here and there. Some of you may appreciate my thoughts, and some of you may cramp up in the afterthought.

A surgeon general's warning is not necessary; however, if you are easily irritated I cannot be held personally responsible for any health related problems that may occur. If at any point you feel your body temperature rising above normal, than close the book, take a deep breath, and get a grip. Mainly I will be exploring the everyday pet peeves that consume a niche in our brain. Sarcasm will be the writing style I have chosen to abuse, thus I can be brutally honest in a comedic sort of way. However, let me point out the fact that I am far from a comedian, and this little error in my genetic make-up makes me prone to the ridicule of those who have chosen to adapt humor as a means of making a living.

Many of the topics I have chosen to write about are just everyday issues that tend to contribute to a lot of controversy. Everything and everyone is prone to a bit of heckling, thus making it sort of a norm in our gracious society. As a matter of fact, many of my topics were spawned from observing the mundane common folk and those who deem themselves a higher power in everyday life.

Numerous people may ask, "Where does this slightly educated, wanna-be author, get of ridiculing everyone else?" Well, the answer my friends lies in the question. I am just an ordinary Joe who is sinking fast into the pit of life. My goals and dreams are very much still alive, but they get further out of reach every day. I do not claim to be greater, smarter, or more successful than the average person. I am not much different than many of you. I have been dealt my hand of cards, and this is how I choose to play them.

Well, enough psycho babble for now. I hope you enjoy my book, and if you don't then you can just add that to your list of everyday grievances that consume your woeful existence. If you do find yourself enjoying the book, then you can refer it to a friend, which will later stimulate further open lines of communication; something that has become so foreign in the land of the free.

PS. I cannot be held accountable for the mechanical errors running through this text. Please try to focus on the contents within versus the imperfections. I hereby give all English teachers the permission to use this book as a format for mechanical do's and don'ts. I've spent many hours dwelling on my *could be* errors, thus I have come to the conclusion that my mistakes are simply supported by my previous claim; being of average intelligence. Thank-you...

TABLE OF CONTENTS

CHAPTER 1

CORPORATE NAZI

They seethe behind their self protective desks, and the only moment of pause is presented by a ritual of barking down orders through the chain of command. The bottom line has now become an obsession, as dollar signs and greed occupy their time budgeted days. I am speaking of the dictators who command the business world, otherwise known as Corporate America.

Many times these folks will start from the bottom and work their way up the corporate ladder. Every step they take, you can almost be sure they are leaving a shoe imprint on a former co-worker. I don't wish to take anything away from these company cheerleaders, such as a dent in their hard-earned education and endless knowledge. I am also not trying to belittle anyone's success, but as one of their peasants this is how I know them.

You see, there are two type of corporate business folk. First there are the cold-conscience mortals who are born with a silver spoon in their mouth. These iron-fisted tyrants are viscous and brutal, having no mercy on an individuals job security. Simply, they are packaged by kindness, but their contents are brimming with arrogance and greed. They possess every material item known to mankind and they always have. Their success in the business world seems almost untouchable because of their glorified title. Who would want to challenge their self-proclaimed superiority, because they uprooted themselves, and they placed their life on the same level as the holy one.

Well wake up and smell the homegrown ladies and gentlemen, because you people need a lesson in reality. I, along with many others, have been your slave for more years than it is worth counting. We come to work on time five days a week, and we stay at least eight hours per day. We obey your every command in hopes of squeezing one more quarter out of that multi-million dollar pocket. You like to call us your family, yet you can't distinguish between who is who, even if we have been employed by you for nearly a decade. God forbid you should take the time to acquaint yourself with those of us who are truly responsible for keeping your business thriving and your customers content. Apparently, "thank-you", is a foreign word in the minds of the CEO's and upper management.

Let's talk about the loyal and dedicated employee for just one moment. Everyday we must greet the grimacing public and maintain a friendly, vivacious perma-grin. When our thick skin shows any sign of elasticity you can be sure the unemployment line has a space with our name on it. You constantly preach about how our welcoming personalities must remain as exhilarating as ever, regardless of how much mental abuse we endure from the gracious consumer. We carry this pride-sucking burden while enduring each and every moment, because we need these jobs. Well Mr. Corporate Brow-beater, without our presence you would literally be accommodated with anal discomfort, while suckling money out of the general public yourself. In your eyes we are merely second rate sludge dregs who should be grateful to be employed by such a prestigious enterprise. However, allow me the pleasure of educating your mind. A majority of your employees exhibit a considerable amount of dislike for you, secretly compare most of the customers to mental patients from an insane asylum, and spend at least five hours per day communicating under our breath about each. The remainder of the time we are pooling our money together to buy the local newspaper for the updated employment ads. Try not to dwell on my obvious exaggerations for too long, because we do wholeheartedly grind the stone when the job demands it. Unfortunately the bills do require payment at some point, so we must work as a necessity to survive. Besides, without people like us who are willing to bottle up our dignity on a regular basis, your stores wouldn't expel such a delightful essence. However, keep in mind that we will only wither in self-pity long enough to catch a ride on the train that tours into the land of fifteen minutes of fame. Now let me take a wild guess at what your ingenious rebuttal to all of this nonsense will be. "You can either move up or move out, but either way you can be replaced."

What a splendid idea...let's omit any ounce of distinction and moral character that resides in our body, for the honor of promotion. The first lesson to climbing the corporate ladder is ascertaining tunnel vision. What I mean by this is without any question you will become the leader of a brainwashed team. If you're starting with a new group you will become the nonpolitical Hitler. The meaning of every word you disgorge will be based on a do as I say and not as I do theory. Due to the high demand of top contender in the human rat race, you will no longer have any true friends within the company. Avoid feeding into the gossip circus, because your own scandalous tattle will become blackmail in a stepping stone for one of your fellow coolies. One last piece of advice. If you attempt to create a thought outside of the big wig handbook, then you should also consider looking for your future replacement immediately.

I worked for a gentlemen one time who proved to be a gifted genius with a knack for the corporate world. He was able to revive even the most dispirited employee, and he firmly supported any person who had a flare in life itself. If a corporate decision was enforced that he deemed injurious to the welfare of his employed, he would address the issue with inventive poise. This man accrued more excellence and respect from his district than I had ever witnessed. The lessons he taught his employees about life and business will be remembered always. However, this same gentleman was terminated because of his will and determination to fight for the slaves in the business. He crossed the boundary between upper management and the hard worker in an effort to extend a caring hand. In the end, his efforts were denied and the empathetic passageway was forever lost. One courageous soul laid his job on the line to fight for the people who link the chain together. Thus, what I along with many others have realized is that the original weak link is located at the very top of the chain. Although the molding is reinforced to withstand

3

massive blows, eventually the shackles will disjoin. Our world is operated by the power of the green eye, and although the mighty dollar may grant you a lot of options during this lifetime, inevitably you will not be allowed to buy your own fate.

Reflect on the decisions you are enforcing today, because someday they may seize you when you least expect it. I must utter one last annotation before I journey to the next aliment.

Instead of assuming the role of clever managerial type, along with consuming our oxygen, try creating a worthwhile policy that you can personally demonstrate. Then, once you have ironed out the kinks, bless us with your presence by appearing in one of your many stores. Then you can demonstrate this new program while giving your employed a first hand look at the value of your bright ideas. Keep in mind that when your first customer of the day literally disposes of his feces on your new suede shoes, you cannot curl up in a fetal position and rock in the corner for the rest of the day. Just grin and bear it, because that is your job.

CHAPTER 2

SERVE YOURSELF

The next subject I will denounce will undoubtedly strike a nerve in both the customer and those involved in public relations. This seems rather appropriate since the theme is relative to that of Corporate Nazi.

After several years in my line of work, I would rather have my eyes gouged out with a cow prod than have to deal with another self righteous customer as long as I live. I know this comes off a bit melodramatic, however, anyone who has ever been on the "May I help you" side of the counter, knows that which I am referring to. Obviously the saying that implies the consumer is always right was created by the one and only customer. Please people, try dwelling a little less on your self-seeking arrogance and concentrate on reality for five minutes.

There are people out there who are so completely oblivious to anything that is going on around them, they would rather act like a complete half-wit than productively use the two fleshy hearing objects located on either side of their underused brain. Most of the time these numbskulls are so busy rattling off at the mouth, by the time they're finished word spewing, they are completely oblivious to their own complaint. You see, this is a customer who enters your establishment fixated on a very petty concern, thus pre-deciding to declare war on the first person who steps into his radar vision. First of all, what people refuse to realize in regard to the customer service industry is that we are granted the permission to compromise in any given situation come hell or high water. That's correct, ladies and gentlemen, you are not required by law to act like a complete hothead over a circumstance that could realistically be resolved in a matter of moments. Apparently during breast feeding at a very over-developed age, a certain handful of over-achievers grasped the theory of intimidation to obtain their desired result. Please do not misinterpret my observations. I am a complete supporter of the theory that advocates securing what you paid for because you worked hard for your money. However, if your video blanks out in the middle of the show, or you get one rotten apple in the bunch, or your CD is cracked before you get it out of the case, don't stomp back into the business and take your whole life's misery out on the one person who bares minimum control. Take it out on the Corporate Nazi.

Imagine for a moment that you are just a regular schmoe trying to do your job the best way you know how, when suddenly you're ensnared in an evil trance by some big tyrant. While standing directly in front of you his jaws of life snaps your head right off the top of your neck. The entire incident probably stemmed from something that could have been handled in a much simpler manner. Again, we are trained to handle a situation if the product does not meet the consumer's satisfaction. The only thing you are accomplishing by freaking out is high blood pressure and a pitch black aura. Not to mention that you have just wreaked havoc on somebody else's day.

The moral of the story is rather simple. Before you open that gaping hole in the lower half of your skull, try communicating with an expression marked by common courtesy. I can guarantee, you will procure the results you expected, and most of the time you will be rewarded a little extra for the inconvenience. Everyone is destined to make a mistake once in awhile, so just imagine what it would be like to have a complete stranger riding your rump every time this lapse of judgement staked a claim on your territory.

There is also the customer who for some apparent reason is under the impression that they are the only patron this planet filled with servers has to attend to. This type A personality wants his service now; case closed. Now Mr. type A, you must come to the realization that we will service you as soon as it is humanly possible. Yes, the four people standing directly in front of you will be waited on a first come, first serve basis. I understand that your time is of great value and people like myself have no business consuming even one precious second. Well, let me clear the air of this thick fog that accompanies your presence, you arrogant fraud. I could care less if you were the leader of the free world. If there are folks waiting in line then you better exhale and take a number, because you don't rate any higher than the welfare recipient standing ahead of you. You will wait and you will enjoy every last minute, or you will find yourself lingering in the checkout of a less tolerant cashier who will be very happy to explain the fundamentals of sharing the same oxygen with people who are truly intolerant of your pitiful existence and your anal calling in life. If you are in that much of a yank than don't place your overpriced stench in our presence. Just hit the gas pedal, and keep on driving. By the way, have a nice day.

Let's flip the coin now, and examine the customer service representative who has no business in this field. I would like to consider myself someone who holds quite a bit of useful knowledge on the issue, only because I have sacrificed my time in this industry for so many years. However, I too have been considered a nasty wench on occasion, simply because I should have been out of the business long ago. It was the pay trap and reckless spending that kept me in, thus I am equal to my own criticism. On the other hand, too many years in this industry will drive even the sanest person over the edge.

First and foremost, I would like to suggest to these type of people that they should consider another line of work. If you are the type of uncivilized person who can barely acknowledge a customer's existence, then get out. If you have a difficult time greeting customers and pretending to enjoy your dutiful employment, then get out. Finally, if you are the type of person who is downright ill-mannered, then take your distemper and utilize it elsewhere. I don't know where barbarians like this get the audacity to be employed in a field where they obviously have no business. Secondly, I would like to meet the schmuck who hired them. I completely understand what it is like to have a putrid day, but you people need to take every ounce of energy within your being and bury your problems until the appropriate time is available. If you just have a naturally foul personality, then seek therapy, because you have no business transmitting your bad vibes to the rest of the public. Not to mention, nobody wants to see your wretched corpse anymore than you want to see ours.

It always amazes me to walk into a business only to find yourself being treated like pond scum. Hey, nobody forced you to apply within, so buck up partner, because without the consumer you have no job. Don't treat us like decomposed cow matter just because life spoiled your dozen eggs. You just remember one thing. The bad day you're having today could ultimately end up being your very last. That one person that you treated like crap could very well be the same person who has you exterminated from your little pit in hell.

To conclude this segment I would like to give a bit of uneducated advice. We were not put on this god-forsaken planet to act like a nuisance to one another. There could not possibly be a problem so global that it would require a gathering of the United Nations. It is not conceivable that the issues we face during a five minute encounter with one another, represent an invitation to a whole day's worth of misery. As for the customer, you should just come in, get what you need, and run along. As far as the representative is concerned, if you don't have what it takes to be civil, then find a career that will tolerate your disposition.

It doesn't take a brain surgeon to figure out the solution to this ordeal. We are not required to relish each other's mere presence, however, we are destined to interact at some point in time. Maybe a little empathy would do us all a bit of good, considering we are supposed to be the representatives of partial maturity while engaging in adulthood. Therefore, in conclusion, if you don't act like a burden on society then you probably wont be treated like one. Thank you and come again.

CHAPTER 3

TUITION TRAUMA

I am going to veer away from any profound moral issues during this chapter. My challenge here is not to focus on values and hardships, but on presumptuous greed.

We have risen above the malicious evils from our past, and now we can embrace the land of the free. Yes, to say the least, I am a bit baffled by a country that abuses the significance of the word free. This overabundance of confusion that preoccupies my mind is more of a twitch. Allow me to get to the point. As we embark on the new millennium we take with us an over capacity of human existence. I can only imagine the amount of intellect that will be deteriorated by the lack of higher education while passing from one century to next.

I am convinced that tuition alone has made a mockery out of the entire school system. How is it possible for the average American jobholder to afford the fruits of our labor, when most of us don't make in a year what the typical degree costs. The government is so fired up about our future generations attending the most prominent schools, yet most of us won't come close for fear of debt beyond our years.

However, don't give up hope just yet. To the surprise of many there are a few options to be considered here. The first alternative would be financial aid. This you can qualify for if you can slip by at least one of the five prerequisites. Let's take a moment to examine a couple of these qualifying determinations. Are you a ward of the court? No, I have parents, and I was raised with a roof over my head. (p.s. if your parents both work you will be disqualified automatically.) Are you single or married? Well I am not exactly single, but I am definitely too immature to be engaged in marital bliss. Finally, do you have any dependants? Well I'll be damned, I don't seem to remember bearing any children in the last twenty some-odd years. Anyway, to make a long story longer, I will unequivocally qualify for financial aid as soon as I get married, pop out a handful of children, and leach off the welfare system. Otherwise the fact remains, as a single, working-class member of society, I could not possibly be worthy of such funds. Wow, that really makes a lot of sense. Every minority under the sun is eligible for financial aid except for the average operative being. A dead carcass gets into college easier than folks like myself.

Now Mr. President, maybe you would like to explain to us what exactly you are planning to do with all of these uneducated mortals festering around your planet. Although I should grant you some credit, because your political dictators are cordial enough to lend us some of money we have been providing to you from our paychecks each and every week. The notorious student loan shows us the payments appear to be quite low, but the interest nearly doubles the original amount after the twenty-year installment plan fizzles out. What a fluke it is to slave so hard for your greenbacks only to find yourself paying oodles of interest on it incognito. Well, I have come to the conclusion that the government is keeping education so far out of reach for the run-of-the-mill character, because if everybody is a rocket scientist then who will pump the gas or serve the food. College is not accessible to many of us because it is not supposed to be. Therefore, I shall tip my hat to those who have slipped through the cracks, thus launching their own success without a college degree. Don't misinterpret my self-involved boohooing, because I am fully aware of how important higher education has become for survival in today's rat race. However, if you happen stumble upon a shortcut, then bravo for your gallant keenness.

I shall not solely reprimand the government for the entire materialization of our upper-level educational facilities. The schools themselves are equally responsible for such calamity. Not to mention how melancholy it is to know that most of our generation is more concerned with the grandeur of the school name rather than what is offered behind the school doors. Post high school pupils are sent forth to a great American learning institution in hopes of grasping the idea of maturity and self-reliability, along with an education. In any case, they are installed with a thousand of their peers, under the same roof, with the guidance of one hall monitor. This multi-cultural living is a four year guarantee to learn a little bit of something and a whole lot of nothing. The one increment of learning they do leave with, besides beer bong mastery and resin lungs, is impeccable social behavior. Let it not remain unspoken that more than half of these students do walk away with some form of degree and diplomacy. However, the fact remains that the amount of time employed in learning versus the amount of time being squandered is the true conflict at hand.

Are we not there to specialize in a particular field of interest? Then I am unclear why it is mandatory to take classes that don't even pertain to the career path which we are striving to achieve. The last time I checked, my manager with a degree in business was not quoting the words from John Quinsy Adams or Robert E. Lee. Yet the class cost him an arm plus his first born, and that didn't even include the books. These colleges and universities can't possibly justify this wasted time even if the most well-known political spokesman is barking for their financial milk bone. We should be demanding that the high schools focus on teaching more of the basic studies, and leave the specific courses up to the colleges and universities. At least then the tax dollars we relinquish yearly could be truly accounted for.

Readers, please lend me your ear. I am not some wigged-out radical who is completely against the works of the entire school system. However, I am discouraged by the opportunity that is rewarded to the select and not equally distributed to all. There are so many people who would give there eyeteeth to attend college, but they refuse to have every penny blindly stripped away. In today's world, college isn't any different than highway robbery. Not only are we being taken by the cost, but the students are deprived of a solid course organized to suit their needs. Instead, we are being forced to render our gross income, and flush it down the toilet for courses we shouldn't have to accept in the first place.

The American people are sightless to so many injustices and choose to remain oblivious. This is our passageway to a better life, yet we would rather turn a blind eye versus fighting for what is ours. Every person productively functioning deserves a fair chance at a higher education, but when the system over indulges in our breadbasket we should have the authority to oppose the right wing prejudice that is railroading our freedom. We can either stop this financially corrupt dilemma, or we can continue to be violated. We better regain control now, because once our education is beyond arms length it will be forever lost. Ignorance is shame, not bliss.

CHAPTER 4

FUR IS DEAD

I would like to dedicate this next chapter to the lives of those who cry silently and mourn brutality throughout unspoken eternity. We hypocritically justify their slavery, thus glamorizing our own ignorance. Their entire existence has been consumed by our need to dominate and conquer. For mankind cannot see through the eyes of the prey, because the spirit inside us all has been shadowed by greed and is thus lying dormant within the aching soul. My words are weightless in such a callous society, but I shall embrace the challenge and moralize until one empathetic being will acknowledge that the end could not possibly justify the means.

Let me begin by saying, fur is dead.

I sit and ponder on the idea of independence and freedom. We as a human race at last concluded that our own existence is more powerful than any other species that may live upon the grounds of this planet. Our pattern of survival has spilled over onto our need to be spoiled and eccentric. Even if that means destroying life to flourish in wealth. Along with its obvious necessary exploitation, fur has become a symbol which the elite employ to authenticate their rank in society. The affluent citizens of our world have made a conscious decision to monopolize the natural environment by wearing dead carcasses simply to gain merit from the rest of the financially-fertile community.

I don't mean to speculate that only the wealthy wear fur. My purpose here is to masterstroke the entire negligence. However, I must use specifics to make a point, so I will designate one population as my experimental guinea pigs, thus empowering them to identify the issue.

I cannot fathom for the life of me why any respectable human being, confessing to hold even one ounce of dignity, would contribute to useless animal slayings. You spend your entire lifetime striving to surpass your own misfortune, ultimately to relish material well being. Knowing that almost every person alive has endured some sort of tragedy at some point, when you then turn around and contribute to something even more gruesome, seems radical. Have the harsh realities of your own lives not given you some sort of compassion towards that which is even less fortunate by its mere existence?

It is rather pathetic to know that our society has become so self absorbed that we can only enjoy the finer fruits of life draped across our bodies. I would think that even the lowest amount of common sense would allow us to understand the difference between extinction and fascination.

Let it not remain unspoken that these egocentric mortals are feeding into the endangered species issue by dumping thousands of dollars into the pockets of the savage stalkers (better known as hunters and trappers). Remember, although you're not participating in the actual killing you are essentially responsible for the last breath of oxygen the animal has taken. By all means, heaven for bid this devastation penetrate your thick-skinned conscience. I am sure you will rationalize your emotionless demeanor through another form of misery. Therefore, in order to make a swift exit on that note I shall leave you with this...

I would like to take a brief moment, and walk you through a day in the life of what you now consider you most valued treasure.

These ravishing creatures are captured in painful, escape resistant, metal clamps that even a human and his ego would have a hard time fleeing from. Many times they are abandoned for days, tormented by agonizing discomfort without any means of food or water. When they are retrieved, this vulgar practice allocates skull bashing until death is fortunate enough to consume their helpless bodies. On other occasions they are shoved into tiny metal cages, and while they are attempting to escape, the force of flailing may snap their necks. If they make it more than a few days, starvation and dehydration exhaust the rest of their strength.

They don't have a name, they are only fur, and fur is dead!

CHAPTER 5

PROLONGING MALE INSANITY:

We are proud to be of the female species, but month after month our bodies become our own worst enemies. You see, one week out of every single month we become a basket case on an emotional roller coaster ride spinning out of control.

I will dedicate this next chapter to the entire male population in hopes of giving you a minor glimpse of what we as the female gender sustain on a regular basis. I don't expect that you can, even for a brief moment, comprehend what we have to endure. You seem to have this perpetual blockage in your brain cells which prevents you from subscribing to any sort of empathy. However, try to excuse yourselves from the feeble mindset that distorts your every thought, and let your brain sponge up my words as though you're reading from your beloved sports column. I will take you on a journey, looking through the eyes of a woman, and perhaps at the end of the cluttered road, evolution will consume your fouled vision of premenstrual syndrome. I will speak in the first person so that you won't get bogged down with the concept of an entire breed. Too much thought only leads to confusion, and I need you to follow this dialogue throughout the entire segment; so stay with me.

In just one week my normal state of mind will succumb to every mood that the human body can support. I continue to read every magazine and book published about the subject of PMS in hopes of finding some relief from the emotional grief that takes away any rational thought. However, as the time creeps upon me, and I have literally exercised every remote possibility, I realize my fate is inevitable. You see, PMS is not a light switch. We cannot just turn it on and off whenever it is convenient. It is also not some lame excuse we have concocted to make your life a living hell. I don't have enough time in the day to concentrate on making you miserable, because I am already consumed by my own anguish.

The dreadful day has come. I know PMS has arrived because the cat food commercial that aired this morning caused me to burst into tears. Today is going to be a very exhausting day because my life is a complete disaster. I have no real friends, I am stuck in a degrading job at a remarkably embarrassing age, and the love of my life is really my enemy. Why does every human that stalks this planet have to take their affliction out on me? I don't care what comes out of your mouth, I know it was meant to be hurtful, and now I am going to bawl uncontrollably. Don't ask me what is wrong, because I have no clue, but what I do know is that I am quite sure it is your fault. Just leave me alone because I hate everything and everyone.

I am sure many of you, both male and female, have experienced or encountered this irrational psycho-babble, weeper. The most amusing craze during this particular phase is that the gentlemen are under the distinct impression that they are the ones who have to suffer through the affair. Here is a reality check for you, my impeccable half-wits. You get to indulge in a mid-life crisis but once in a lifetime, whereas we get to participate in the festivities once a month. Let me tell you, by the time we do reach menopause, most of us will be heading towards loonyville anyway. You should feel fortunate if we don't take you with us. I am sure you are drifting off at this point so let me take you right into phase two.

I wake up in the morning feeling sparkling and refreshed from a good night's sleep. I stroll down the stairs and I see the love of my life positioned upright in the makeshift Lazyboy. Suddenly the words "Honey, would you mind refilling my cup of coffee while you're out there please?" come spewing out of his mouth. Instantly I am ticked off, and it was definitely due to his endless loafing and patronizing tone of voice. (I am going to veer away from men understanding the tone of voice theory, because no matter how many times you try to explain it, their rusty thinker just doesn't want to leave neutral.) Anyway, what does he mean, can I pour him another cup of coffee? I don't see any crutches. His legs appear to be in good working physical condition. He better stay far away from me for the rest of the morning, because I have had it up to here. Depending on how I am feeling, I might return his head by tomorrow. In any case, I am already in a foul mood and it is only 8:30 am. I will not put up with any crap from people today, because I am already feeling provoked and annoyed. If I encounter any offensive human contact directly, I am bound to gouge out somebody's eyes with all twenty of my nails. If you think I am kidding then I dare you to bother me. I'll be scraping eye parts out from underneath my toenails for the next two days. It will be a very good day if I haven't been incarcerated by nightfall.

It is very hard to determine which of the two phases offers the most damage to your everyday existence. The cry-over-anything phase is very destructive to your pride and self-esteem. The feeling of complete anxiety weighs on your every thought and every move without alleviation. Making it through an entire day, tear-free, is an accomplishment in itself. The only thing you can hope for is compassion from those who are closest to you.

However, the second phase is the most earth-shattering of the two. This facet could be catastrophic on your social well being, because you're like a walking time bomb. Those who are closest to you will most likely perceive you as being a pacing nightmare and will make any effort to keep their distance. In any case, making a quick recovery after the week is over, undoubtedly is you ticket to a safe return.

Therefore, it is vital for you as the male species to at least pretend to sympathize with us, though it may do you more harm than good. Yes, if you haven't figured it out by now this is a no-win situation for you.

Therefore in return I will agree that men do absorb the superficial potency of our overactive hormones. However, you are able to turn around and walk away, whereas our only escape is sleep cycle number three. Believe me when I say that we don't enjoy trying to function during this psychotic tour of emotions.

Thus, having someone of the opposite gender belittling our every move only provokes an antipathetic ambiance. In any case, your only safe house is a complete evacuation from the planet earth, or just a bit of silent understanding and patience might suffice.

On the other hand, if you elect to disregard everything that I have written, and choose to utter a sarcastic remark about PMS, you may want to arm yourself with a protective cup. Here is a bit of advice. Take your corrosive words and stick them where the sun doesn't shine, because if you don't, we will. Midol, take me away...

CHAPTER 6

ABANDONING OUR CREATION

Mother Nature is our womb, and we as the human race are her birth defect. We have been on the planet earth for a legion of centuries, therefore, you would anticipate that every generation would progress in protecting and conserving our beloved domain. However, our ability to neglect and pulverize to satisfy our day-to-day survival has out-weighed our loyalty to the one parent who will ultimately demolish our existence. Mother Nature is running out of patients with mankind, and inevitably she will adjudicate our destiny as a living species. Do not assume that the sentence she imposes on us will be any more cordial than the destruction we have wreaked on her native grounds. Although we haven't already expended our own duration, our carefree persistence will be evident in the final outcome leading to condemnation. We are completely oblivious to our own extinction because our longevity is considered invincible through our own lack of rational thought. We are at war with our protector and forfeiting the battle of our own destiny. The real dilemma that seems to linger is based on whether or not Mother Nature progresses in destroying us, or will she remain composed until we wreak havoc on our own immortality?

Let us take a moment to dissect the question that may very well ration our necessities for life. Will Mother Nature ultimately emerge as our universal gravestone?

Every day is a routine marked by human ignorance. Flocks of communities evacuate there homes as a custom while their personal belongings succumb to the destruction of a natural disaster. When misfortune has passed, souls will once again habitat the grounds and materialization will commence. Mortals will forge ahead until another slap in the face inflicts devastation on their well-being.

It's time to initiate a new trend which will call for the removal of all rose-colored glasses sported by the human culture. Doesn't it seem rather apparent that Mother Nature is not toying around with some obsessive prank for the mere purpose of capturing our attention for a brief moment? The mayhem that has been delivered to us so far is perhaps rather effortless compared to the devastation that may be in store for our future.

I am not seeking out some miraculous cure which will prove to solve all world problems, I am simply a messenger trying to highlight an entire rash of lifelong delinquencies. We are destroying our fetal bio-dome by cutting off our own umbilical cord. The rivers that flow through this land are the veins of our foundation. We are injecting fatal poison into these veins, and we voluntarily persist with all disregard to consequence. If you are waiting for the future Einstein to concoct a supernatural antidote for this manmade, contaminated, burial ground, then you are banking on a very distorted vision. How can we leave this picturesque country with toxic impurity soaking in every pore?

We can no longer close our eyes to this consensual noxious behavior. If we as a nation, as a human race, and as an entirety, don't stop this manufactured destruction immediately, come decades down the road we may be left to survive with very few options. We must not wait to be reprimanded by catastrophe for the consequences will prove to be unmerciful. Through our own lack of thought we will completely disintegrate our entire future, and the future of those who will never be given the opportunity to help mend the ill-treatment of our empire.

On the other hand, Mother Nature may be the least of our worries at this point. With the population swelling at a colossal rate, the need to annihilate one another for complete domination will perhaps triumph over any natural assault. Human instinct thrives on the mentally hypnotic suggestion to secure self worth and a niche in this preconceived, mapped out, itinerary of life. The universal goal is to leave an impressionable legacy during the course of a lifetime, but with so much competition the predecessor becomes the adversary, and the enemy must be assassinated. We no longer thrive on compassion and unity, because we have become evil-minded through fear and revenge.

How very dispiriting it is to know that a mass population full of variety can work so diligently to eliminate one another instead of collaborating as a whole. The global energy that is squandered through fueling hatred could be combined with the slowly depleting resources for an unforeseen plague of unknown proportions.

Unfortunately at some point in time history always manages to repeat itself. Our species is becoming too injurious because that is what benefits us for the time being. Once upon a time the boundary between good and evil was created. When the line is crossed by the majority through an eruption of tainted decisions, a higher power will contaminate mankind through mental insanity or physical deterioration. When the moment comes we will become entangled in our own destructive web which will propel us into extinction. We are all given one opportunity to act humane, but again and again we choose to walk the path of inevitable abolishment.

It is sobering to know that we have been given two opportunities to interact, yet we have deserted both avenues. We were given this remarkable world within the solar system to nurture. Instead we maim and abuse every inch until there is nothing left for our personal gain. Mother Nature can regenerate after we nearly destroy her, but first we must be removed from her dismembered grounds. You would not allow somebody to enter your home with the intention of inflicting total destruction, and neither will she. There is no force stronger than that of a natural creation, regardless of how advanced technology becomes. We are on the verge of a systematic global breakdown that will consume both the compassionate and the corrupt. Our glorious mother is at a breaking point, and when she makes the decision to abort the disease called the human race, it will surely be a day of total retribution for her. The only sign of our time will be the scars we leave behind. Mother Nature can heal, but extinction cannot.

Finally, our second chance at existence has been diluted by universal dementia. We are so far beyond equilibrium that even the children have been placed in this war. We have now traded our loathing for one another over physical appearance in exchange for an even greater amount of illogical thought. We are falling into one big melting pot of hatred and taking anyone, regardless of age, color, or gender. We are a dying breed being strangled by the clutches of our own hands. Soon we will be coming to a fork in the road. At an extremely irrational speed we will be faced with two choices, and each will result in our expiration. The first road will lead us directly into the devouring destruction of Mother Natures wrath, or we can diverge into the left appendage where we will suffer a bitter execution driven by the hatred of our own species. Though it is not an easy decision to make, it is the pattern we are molding for our future.

It is quite possible that even the most indigestible statements will have a very minor effect on intentionally deaf ears. People will not acknowledge how much we're taking advantage of this beautiful creation. The world is so precious, yet most folks sprint through life using tunnel vision rather than seeing how fortunate we are to be surrounded by the mystical and fantastic animation of the planet earth. For heaven sakes, just take one moment out of your corroded lifestyles and realize how blessed we all are that fate has brought us to live in such a spectacular habitat.

Material possessions do not make you a truly rich person. You can only obtain an infinity of wealth by appreciating the true nature of life and the environmental surroundings that are offered with it. Even if we have reached a point of no return, hopefully someday our souls can be exonerated through global forgiveness. Although we have stifled her, I truly believe that Mother Nature will eventually reside in tranquillity and free of animosity. She will shine again one day. Therefore, let us concentrate on creating peace with ourselves, with each other, and most of all with our biological Mother Earth.

CHAPTER 7

KEEPING IT IN YOUR PANTS

We are bound by the laws of marriage, and together we will overcome any obstacle that poses a threat to our sacred bond. The love we share between us is so pure and powerful that our souls unite to create an energy that is forever undivided. My intimate spirit is kindled by the touch of your hand, and your impassioned whisper illuminates my aura. Together our mind, spirit, and souls overflow with a consecrated promise held together by trust, love, and complete devotion to one another. You are my knight in shining armor brought down from the heavens to share this mystical dream come true. I love you everlastingly, and forever we will be.

Love is the most rewarding gift that can be shared between two people, and I shall ultimately not displace the beauty of that special intimacy. However, we are losing sight of that significance, so I must start by focusing on the heartache and grief that is caused by the broken promises. My first paragraph describes the sanctuary of true love, but sometime thereafter betrayal emerges to devour this spoken trust. The words we declare are so meaningful and true, yet it makes you wonder at what point does it all come crashing down? Then I will attempt to portray the virtual radiance of unconditional love, and how trivial it has become in today's society.

In a perfect romance portrayed fictitiously are those who exist for the purpose of finding their true love, and through those expectations we ultimately relate this sense of falsehood to our own everyday lives. This bit of excellence that is fed to us is often misinterpreted through physical actions instead of raw emotion. In any case, this will generally lead to one's brain being masterminded by their muscle, and unfortunately the expressway to love becomes a quick detour into a bleak sorrow. You see, speaking in general terms, there are two kinds of people who seek out their own rendition of love. The first variety of species is emotionally tied to a relationship, and physically drawn to act on the lure of seduction. These road whores are like a magnet for the vulnerable. They stalk submissive females who are overcome by personal anguish or naïve, and they draw them into a world of artificial amour. Their perfection seems unyielding, and they will show you an affection that is foreign to you. When you act out your every fantasy, and fully allow them to discover your entire psyche, they suddenly cease to exist. This female fancier who swept you off your feet is an emotional thief who is continually justified by a desperate frame of mind. As long as there is someone to feed into his reckless ego, he will continue to wreak impairment on a girl's weak self-esteem. The only way to seek closure after this narrow-minded barbarian has imposed agony on you, is to prevail beyond your sorrow, and evolve into self-fulfilled enlightenment.

Now I realize your mind and body are surrendering to every aching emotion, but you must come to reconcile your own misfortune for the sake of closure. Although you may struggle with the notion of being played for a fool, the real victim evolves from those who will not allow themselves to continue on. The agony that once ruled you is now compounded with the loss of a fictitious Romeo. You have cavorted with a Casanova who is off hunting his next prey. Your first step in recovery from this emotional ruin is self-discovery. You must realize that although you were deceived by a philanderer, within your depths lies a profound and captivating beauty that will emerge beyond the shadow of all hopelessness. I am not a psychiatrist who is free to pass out advice, but through experience I do know that if you don't acquire inner strength from your first misfortune, then surely you are prone to becoming a casualty of deceptive love once again. There is no guarantee in life, but benefiting from both experience and knowledge will assist in creating your resistance to duplicity. Take advantage of time, because it is the healer of all anguish. Become one with your inner spirit so you can be wise hereafter to this type of dysfunctional sociopath.

Unfortunately, while you're recuperating during this period of triumph over tribulation, Mr. Hot Pants is probably fixating on another lost soul. However, while he is engaged in further sexual, adulterous, misdemeanors, his alienated companion is anxiously awaiting the arrival of her dishonest prince. Here lies another baffling dilemma. It seems to me that you would have to bear some sort of female intuition that your mate is a compulsive swindler. The problem is that these females are so taken in by this fictitious romance that their mind is completely befuddled with denial. This gambler who is declaring his undying love for you is playing Russian Roulette with you life and the lives of his present day flings. The only piece of advice I can possibly offer is for you to seek professional counseling so that you can obtain enough self-worth to open the door and run like the wind. Don't look back because all you will see is a contaminated wiener, and a fraudulent way of life.

Ok, now let me take a moment to address the hail Mary nympho. I realize your entire existence is driven by the need to be permanently fondled, but when you start railroading other people's self-importance and their right to life, then you have consciously overstepped the boundary that represents mutual trust. All you are really enacting is a low budget portrayal of a worthless exhibitionist who will wake up one morning only to realize your family jewels are on the verge of decay. Gosh, what will you do when you're permanently out of commission, and dear mother thumb along with her four sister fingers risk jerking it right off your body. I wouldn't suggest looking for companionship, because no one will want to play with your infected recreational novelty. Well, you dickless wonder, I just hope a few years of foolish promiscuity is worth a lifetime of solitude.

Believe it or not there is another side of the male species, littering erupting with moral dignity and virtue. These guys are as down to earth as the breed allows. Many times their physical appearance may not be molded into a picture perfect package, but they are truly authentic right down to their fundamental seed. They will pamper and court a lady in a manner that literally distinguishes them from the rest of their gender. Ironically enough, these gentleman are always manipulated by unsophisticated women who can't appreciate an honest and genuine demeanor. A vast amount of women have corroded priorities, so undeniably, with them, beauty only runs skin deep. These guys are temporarily good for the convenience of the moment, but they are eventually treated equivalent to yesterday's trash. This holds true because unfortunately these guys have been branded with the *nice guy* image, which makes them too elementary compared to the challenge of taming a superficial whore. I can only tell you that these magnificent humans are a lifeline for people who desire sincere adoration, not a scratching post for kittens who belong in a completely different litter box all together. Since the world is fouled by so much duplicity, it is very difficult for bona fide soul mate seekers to discover one another. However, if you stay true to yourself without selling out to a majority of society's corruptive behavior, the accomplishment will ultimately grant the reward.

In closing I would like to point out that clearly both men and women are equally capable of engaging in scandal. We are all faced with temptation at some point in time, but there is a heroic difference between those who choose to masquerade, and those who remain loyal to their sole companion. We are all naïve to the expression of love, and unfortunately there are those who shamefully misuse the concept to their advantage.

For those of you who are making a mockery out of loyalty and adoration, I can only hope that you experience the same affliction that you are so lightheartedly dishing out. I realize that as we embark on a new era , life and times will change, but just like the quality of life, it is crucial for some things to remain a high moral priority. Statistics for divorce are at an all time high because people have chosen to make sexual intercourse a fascinating hobby instead of a special intimate moment shared exclusively between two people. Instead of entering into a marriage like it's a frivolous high school relationship, take just one moment to realize that the words you're declaring in your vows to one another are supposed to be a true expression from the depths of your soul. If you can't acknowledge this fact then have enough respect for yourself and for your spouse to get a grip and terminate the relationship before you institutionalize conjugal suicide. Whatever demons may be governing your image of the opposite sex, at least maintain enough dignity to confront your past before you initiate a hidden agenda of self-destructive behavior. I have never witnessed anyone declare that they wanted to be the central support system for sexually transmitted diseases. However, when you make judgements solely operating off the brain in your pants instead of utilizing the common sense stemming from the organ in your skull, then you're inadvertently aiming towards that goal.

For those of you who envision that true love exists, please continue to embrace that concept. Although the world is filled with a collection of chaos and unscrupulous activity, there are still those who thrive on loyal and undisguised companionship while abstaining from the mind games. These notable figures do not constitute a majority of the population, however, once cupid unites two of a kind nothing will destroy what they can build together. Hold on to your dreams, because karma and fate will work simultaneously to bring you to a special place in life which most people admire from a far. Remember that your heart is like a rainbow, and if you follow it to the end you will most definitely find your pot of gold. Your brain is the leader of choice, but your heart is the always the leader in love. Don't cheat yourself out of that chance of a lifetime.

CHAPTER 8

DON'T DILLY-DALLY, JUST DRIVE

I am going to simplify these next few pages by merely pointing out that there are those who deserve the privilege of motoring, and those who should consider suspending their own freedom to drive. It's not really up to each individual by mere preference who should be on the cemented route system and who should not. This would only lead to very deserted roadways. However, when the issue of safety factors in as an overall problem, then it's time to re-evaluate an individual's capability, both physically and mentally. Now, unless the Secretary of State is in cahoots with the automobile industry, it is very disturbing to see all of the incompetent drivers mingling with all of those who associate common sense as a prerequisite for operating a piece of equipment that could annihilate anyone coincidentally coursing the same path. I hereby give this chapter to all legal drivers as another piece of useless jargon to adapt as their theoretical piece of mind. The three types of drivers that will be revealed do not render the entire population, however, a majority may find that they do fit the description of one or more of these characteristics listed. Consider this chapter as you will, however, keep in mind that without depicting each individual's highway compulsions, whether skillful or otherwise, the entire issue may never have the opportunity to experience resolution.

First of all, let me direct your attention to the petite, square shaped, black and white, bold lettered, MPH indicator, sitting slightly away from the side of the road. Surprise, this strange inanimate object does serve a purpose. At least as far as I know it wasn't designed to symbolize roadway décor. In any case, if you are already perplexed by my lingo, I am referring to the infamous speed limit sign which is commonly posted on the shoulder of the street, highway, freeway, road, expressway, or whatever you feel the need to call it. I am attempting to be a little over-descriptive because I would bet my left arm that at least fifty percent of the population is truly oblivious to the logic behind regulating mobile velocity. Let me introduce you to the first scenario.

You're driving along minding your own business, when all of a sudden, a vehicle from out of the blue pulls right out in front of you. Not only has this cretin failed to realize that the opposing traffic could be detrimental to his duration here on earth, but now Mr. Head in the Clouds decides to drive 10mph under the speed limit. Immediately you become baffled by his complete ignorance and disrespect towards other drivers, therefore you exercise a great American tradition by flipping him the bird.

I just want to say to these types of drivers that not only should you avoid engaging in any sort of operative automobile activity for security reasons alone, but your lack of common sense in general should ultimately earn you the right to a free annual drivers training course until you become one with at least three of your five senses. Granted anyone with an ounce of sane judgement becomes in charge of the office which issued you your drivers license in the first place. Let me sum this up by saying that if you can't drive faster than a land turtle strung out on speed, then do us all the favor of staying home, or better yet try experiencing the joys of carpooling. Secondly, if you are unable to be fully aware of your entire surroundings at all times, then you will inevitably become road kill. Keep in mind that in definition this does not only describe dead animal carcasses.

In fair play, while I am dwelling on the whole speed limit issue, I must also address those of you who think the limitation of speed is defined by how high the speedometer in your car reaches. Your ability to weave in and out of traffic so gracefully will eventually make you customer of the year in the eyes of the automobile insurance industry. I myself enjoy the rush of speeding, however, there are those of you who need to consider joining acceleration anonymous. These are the type of people who adapt thinking as an after-the-fact criteria. Therefore, let me escort your mind into scenario number two.

Again, you're driving along on a peaceful afternoon when unexpectedly the opposing traffic is now in your lane, trying to pass a gargantuan size eighteen wheeler, and dodging straight towards you. Of course in this situation there is no time to expedite the traditional hand gesture, because death is looming in your near future.

First and foremost, let me just say that if a I had a bionic arm I would reach out my car window, and slap your face off for having the audacity to put my life in the palms of your hands. Listen here, you imprudent freak-aholic, if you are in that much of a yank to get somewhere, then pick up the telephone and let the waiting party know that you have decided against killing ten people in order to get to your destination on time. I can adhere to a little excess acceleration, but it's crucial to remain within reason. Negligently taking someone out does not fall in that category. Not to mention how the moment will embrace solitude when you have to explain to the families of the victims why another five minutes was the difference between life, death, and arriving at the exact moment.

Last but not least, I would like to dispatch the final leg on the triangle, so let's take a look at one more idea. Thus far I have lectured on and leaped from one extreme to the next, yet there still seems to be one more angle of speed lingering on the road. These people are the true definition of saints according to the enforcement officers of the highway law. They follow the speed limit right down to the exact mark, not budging until the sign gives them the right of way. I would like to tip my hat to these impeccable beings, however, to belly up on hypocrisy you are the ones who tap dance on the feeling of irritability the most. I am not going to offer a scenario during this instance, because your actions are clearly self explanatory. You see, I truly believe that you can sort of taunt the speed limit by going slightly over the minimum posted. Unless of course you enter upon a residential area, because in this case you could ultimately end up becoming liable for one of the many unattended children traipsing around. Anyway, the point is, if you're on the highway and the speed limit is posted at 55 mph, it's really acceptable to drive maybe around say...61 mph. I only feel the need to mention this because the mental energy flowing from the twenty five tailgating drivers behind you appears to be some sort of negative vibe gathering in the atmosphere. Yet the obviousness stemming from this situation could be painfully clear due to the scowl across each of their faces. It is better to remain in the flow of traffic than to rehash some childhood fantasy of the tortoise and the hare. This may very well prevent a lot of erratic driving from the rest of the motorists. Let me conclude by saying that I am fully aware that you abide by the law to avoid a ticket, but I can almost guarantee the police will not incarcerate you for very slight vehicular rebelliousness. Therefore let me just remind you that the gas pedal is on the right, and to maneuver more rapidly you must press down with a little bit of firmness beyond what you are used to. It is a rather simpleton like execution, just don't panic, whatever you do.

Finally, I would like to sum up this entire chapter by spewing out a few words of wisdom. Our society is inherently consumed by fury and anger towards one another. Although I have made light of the situation at hand, it is becoming a very dangerous issue in today's world. People are literally crossing the line of sanity over someone else's driving habits. When the big picture is painted with violence because more people need Ritalin than not, then it is time to step back and re-evaluate the situation in its entirety. Road rage is dominating over the majority because people have become too self-righteous in their own meager existence, frazzled by the pressure of daily life. I don't care how horrendous an individual's driving habits are, it's even more appalling to witness an execution over something so insignificant. If you are the type of person who becomes over-enraged simply by the naïve misjudgment of another, then seek some sort of hypnotic therapy. If I die at the hands of another motorist over a slight mishap, then I swear by everything that holds true to me, I will return as a ghost and haunt you into eternity. It's becoming mandatory that we find a solution to this travesty very quickly. If we do not resolve this issue then the government may as well start operating a homicide lottery, because it is just one more place in this world that will succumb to the evil of a human's pent up ferocious energy. If you can't handle the responsibility of driving, which includes both physical and mental capability, then either hitch a ride or check yourself into a psycho ward. However, don't burden the rest of us with your neurotic tendencies. Remember to buckle up, it's the law!

CHAPTER 9

INDEPENDENTLY OWNED AND OPERATED

During this chapter I would like to set aside condemning or condoning any malicious act created by our species, and focus on the inner self. I truly believe that the personal contact we make between one another sort of outlines the foundation of our being. Therefore, instead of dwelling on the external cause and effect of our physical actions, I would rather sink deeper into the soul and deliver an in-depth look at the personage within in order to understand the conduct that distinguishes each individual from the next. The majestic human culture is so grand that it is not feasible for me to individually portray the characteristics that compose a complex structure, filled with feelings and emotions, to create the cosmetics of one's self. Therefore, I would like to take you on a brief excursion parceling two very dissimilar personalities. However, you must realize that I am locked into using very general terms, thus concluding that I will only be portraying one's selfhood through communal cognizance and personal scrutiny. Therefore, only a small percentage of the population may be able to identify and connect with my particular theories regarding individuality. However, my goal is to supercede the universal attitude of placing judgement upon others, and allow you to employ empathy for the distinguishing traits these two personalities have to offer. Let me unveil the mystery of the silent and the unreserved. During the first segment I will be speaking in both the first and second person, only because I have immediate familiarity with the silent ones. However the second passage will be filled with a non-bias viewpoint originating from direct observation of the population. In any case, let's begin.

When a flock of busybodies emerge, there will be at least one individual who will barely engage in any sort of conversation with the rest of the clan. These people are typically recognized as the silent ones. Quiet people are often misinterpreted because we are not proficient at bouncing around from person to person, assuming the role of Chatty-Cathy. People who don't declare vocal adaptability are usually categorized as being self-righteous snobs, all the way to the extreme of uneducated morons. People like us feel much more at ease being approached with conversation rather than being the instigator of intellectual chat. It's not because we deem ourselves as being on an untouchable pedestal, or that we're completely foreign to our inherited dialect. It's just when it comes down to it we have no skills at speaking on an interesting topic that requires more than a yes or no answer. Now I am sure this will lead a lot of pseudo psychiatrists to conclude that we lack self-esteem and the necessary social adaptability that is mandatory to survive in society. Although this theory may release a smidgen of accuracy, as sort of an oxymoron, quiet people are by far some of the most interesting people you will ever have the opportunity to encounter. You see, we basically have this all-around knowledge of the common world through mere observation. Our outlook feeds off from the remainder of energy exhausted by those who spend most of their day trying to be the center of attention. Although being outspoken would be beneficial in unavoidable situations, for the most part we just want to remain professionally latent. I don't expend a great deal of energy towards being gregarious mainly because I would rather focus my energy in another area of my mental domain. Quiet people have such fascinating and profound outlook on the entire meaning of existence, that we take the time to appreciate the things that most people deem as insignificant. We have the ability to expose our puzzle-like personalities one piece at a time, until you put together a meaningful picture complimented by variety and distinctive coloring. Scholars of tranquility desire acceptance for who they are instead of being obligated to fill a pair of ill-suited shoes society has created for them. Therefore, the next time you're in an atmosphere with a variety of people, take the initiative to affiliate yourself with the self-effacing wallflower. I can almost guarantee they will walk you through a spectacular array of perpetual intrigue. Therefore, embrace me for who I am rather than trying to manufacture me into a flawless representative of social perfection.

Now, let me direct your attention to socially appraised personality dues. I truly admire every individual who has the ability to mingle in any given situation. These are the type of folks who have become professional experts at the art of social well-being. You are able to sway in and out of crowds without being the least bit inhibited. Bravo for your chit chat skills, and may your social expertise remain with you always. Without these types of people convivial gatherings would rank in the essence of sterile. Let's face it, these mortals bring life to any entertainment festivity. Their personal needs are set aside only to cast about a collection of immediate response in the form of laughter. The only self-destructive image these people may contend with is the occurrence of solitude. The word in itself is completely foreign to their dialect. Society has burdened them so much with the idea of acceptance, that even the mere speculation of being detached from the human culture is enough to drive them into emotional senselessness. The expectations that have been placed upon them during every hospitable encounter must provide enough stress to initiate mind boggling hallucinations of social deprivation. Don't misconstrue my speculation. I am not maintaining that these folks are sulking in misery. I just want the public to allow these people to become one with their personal substance. If you are going to burden them with these types of expectations, at least have the courtesy of passing around a collection tray, and pay them for their services rendered.

I wanted to bring to your attention these specific personalities so that society could have a more open view of the paramount distinctions between the two. Most people will flock to what is approved in the eyes of the majority, and that alone tends to feed into an enterprise of unforeseen prejudice that whisks through the environment like a foul aroma. Everyone is plagued with a personality flaw, so it seems we should embark on a more definite theme of pure acceptance rather than shy away from what is not simple, clear-cut, and familiar. This topic may seem rather frivolous to some of you. Yet to those of us who have to endure annoying ridicule by those who transparently suffer from flawless personality syndrome, it is paramount that I bring this to your attention. My point is that even those who appear to be without character default have to obscure their own insecurities through the use of other people. Regardless of whichever distinguishing traits partition us from one another, it is clear that every person has something unique to offer this world. Whatever makes you comfortable in your own skin is what will inevitably guarantee your own true happiness, whether it's being reserved or otherwise. In any case, if you stay true to yourself without selling out to how other people label your actions, in the end you will be able to stand pure and proud for the person you are defined by your own expectations. Regardless of the change this world inherits, the one bad habit people can't disembarrass is the outward criticism of one another. If you define your life solely on the faultfinding commentary of others, you will eventually come to the realization that your own existence and self-worth is foreign to your mind and spirit. The most important aspect of life you can take with you into eternity is an inner strength that leaves a luminous aura around your soul.

CHAPTER 10

HAPPY HAPPY HEMP JOY

As a feature of our past this drug is now considered a devil worshiper's lifeline. This is how anybody on the straight and narrow would describe what I once considered the next best thing to hypnotherapy. I will be completely up front and honest. I am not a foreigner to the entrancing relish of marijuana, however, to be politically correct I must attempt to tap dance on the path of the clean and sober. The key word is attempt, and considering my use of the word political I am left wide open to an arena bursting with indecisiveness. In any case, if this particular cigarette ever becomes legal again, we might be able to suspend our need to destroy and annihilate one another by exchanging our negative energy and replacing it with artificial tranquility. At the same time, total logic meltdown may ease the rupture of our vast and relentless technology. I don't really have any miraculous point to spew during this chapter, I just wanted to spark a little fire under your rumps just in case you started daydreaming about this morning's multigrain cereal bar eaten only to recover from my previous whacked out viewpoints. Therefore I must seize your undivided attention while misplacing your logical thinking that separates right from wrong, and I come to the conclusion that obtaining this goal can only be accomplished by embracing the wonders of a native herb. Don't misconstrue my intelligence for that of a drug pusher, because I am not a candidate in the pro choice weed campaign, however, I will not denounce those who choose to enjoy the essence of pot. It would take me through the next millennium to do so considering I know more people who smoke the drug than not. I have engaged in the festivities myself so I must be very cautious not to overstep that fine line of hypocrisy. Basically I would like to cover a few points of interest about a drug that is under a great deal of scrutiny. Therefore I will not continue to bore you with my useless chatter, and in order for that reality to surface you must allow me to guide you on journey that entails a bit of idle logic.

First and foremost, I would like to analyze the medical controversy surrounding marijuana, for it tends to lead to universal and thought provoking negatives concerning this illegal contraband. From what I understand according to the anti-herbal fault finders of America, is that weed leads to the use of more oppressive drugs, and it induces short term memory damage. Let's take a moment to manifest that polluted narrative. Presuming that marijuana leads to the use of heavier drugs is in itself misleading. That would be like saying alcohol leads to smoking cigarettes, and nicotine escorts the mind into the world of diluted substance abuse. As the saying goes, guns don't kill people, people kill people. Hang in there it's the same concept. Secondly, I will bow to the government favored statistic that unmasks the effect marijuana has on short term memory. However, this side effect seems a bit insignificant compared to the upshot that circumstances many of the available prescription drugs that are legal and readily available. Therefore, I do not feel these claims are a legitimate defense in the condemnation of this meditative ground plant. (More recent studies will probably prove me to be completely wrong, but whatever)

Many of our hippie folks from the sixties and seventies engaged in pot smoking affairs, and many of these same inhabitants became successful in life's journey. Although they participated in this well known social gala, it does not mean their memory was affected to the point of paralysis. Pot may result in a bit of short term recollection retardation, but we will still have moments to reminisce about when age and decrepitude consume us.

At this point I am quite taken back by what is legal and what is considered a complete penetration of the entire judicial system.

I would like to describe in variance, for those of you who have never hop scotched over to the wild side, the effect pot has on your overall perception of life. Immediately after toking on the homegrown cigarette you have this overwhelming sense that the world has suddenly become a Mary Poppins playground, while embracing perfection, thus sparing zero tolerance for any fault. Your entire environmental surroundings are presented in a fashion that emulates touring through the land of perpetual amusement, and all the little entities that go hand I hand with life couldn't be more hysterical if laughter was the only reaction known to man. The word stress has no bearing on your physical and emotional being because you have evoked a more visual state of consciousness.

I am not going to completely glamorize marijuana because during and after the peculiar buzz a few down falls take precedent. During the initial high some people have the tendency to become rather paranoid. My theory (which stems from personal experience alone and is not supported by any scientific legitimacy) is that your mind has momentarily shifted itself into panic mode due to fear of the unknown. Your body isn't necessarily physically reacting to your state of mind, meaning that you're not curled up under your bed in the fetal position waiting for the boogie monster to attack, but the expression on your face will be a tell tale sign. The THC in weed does not acquaint itself with your mind in the form of a hallucinogen, you're simply experiencing an emotional reaction. This does not factor in as the entire experience, it just happens to be an occasional malfunction.

The second and most ghastly consequence dopers will encounter is the infamous munchy stage. I wouldn't recommend an overabundance of weed to those of you who are trying to pinch an inch. Not only will you most likely disregard any form of control and exercise, but you may very well eat yourself out of house and home. You see, after smoking weed your sense of taste becomes considerably heightened. As a matter of fact, there isn't much that couldn't satisfy this craving.

Buyer Beware! Never treat yourself to a grocery store rendezvous during an elevated buzz. If you decide to embark on this journey you should prepare yourself with a credit card in one hand and a minimum of two friends who are willing to escort you on this train of carts parade. The grocery store is like a destiny date with the lottery jackpot, and if you're not careful you may find yourself buying the equivalent of just that.

Now, I have just described to you in detail the effects of an illegal substance, so in fair play I must also evaluate a legal drug of our day. When you blossom into full-fledged adulthood at the age of 21, your drivers license becomes the ticket that permits you into the drinking saloons. With this plastic permission you have access to alcohol until you're at the point of gross inebriation. During your first couple of drinks you begin to feel lighthearted and content. However, this gratification soon trades itself in for oblivion, and your entire sense of perception becomes null and void. Unfortunately you soon find yourself unfamiliar with how many drinks you've consumed, and your entire equilibrium is thrown into a frenzy. Your tongue becomes a paperweight for your jaw, so the sentence fragments that sputter from your mouth in a slow motion dialect make perfect sense to the guy standing next to you with his tongue sitting on the barstool beside him. By the end of the merry making cartel you find your new best friend is hard, moist, and cold with the universal nickname of porcelain god. Low and behold, by 5 p.m. the next evening your stomach problems begin to reside, and the intense construction work inside your head has finally gone into temporary layoff. Last but not least, you swear to god that you will never ever drink again as long as you live, or at least until next weekend rolls around.

Well, slap my face and call me stupid, now I understand why alcohol is legal and marijuana is not. An overdose of alcohol in the system is like playing Russian Roulette, it can kill you. Too much weed will put you to sleep, because it is impossible to smoke to death in one night. I am once again going to teeter on that caution boundary, and challenge this thesis as being a government conspiracy better known as population control. The political state of our demise is always based on a hidden agenda. Let it not remain unspoken that I would encourage people to smoke marijuana before I would favor an alcohol binge and purge. Therefore, running for political office has been expelled from my future career roadway because I did inhale.

Although I am making light of the situation at hand, I do realize that a large segment of the human culture categorizes this drug with any other. To a legion this is an altercation that spares little tolerance for dispute. However, on the other hand, where the grass is much much greener, the only contention is wrongful incarceration for an inferior misdeed.

Finally, if you choose to remain substance free, then I shall offer you my sincere congratulations, but don't reprimand those who enjoy a gift from the ground. I am not proclaiming that we should all sprint to the streets and start abusing drugs of any kind. Marijuana ranks in an entirely different class compared to the evils that are controlling the minds of the weak. We live in an addiction society that rebels against all social limitations, and from that alone we tend to scurry towards a solution that provides minimum results. The justification that we have provided through legalities only satisfies a temporary need for logical answers to a universal problem that is blindsiding our ability to regain control. If you're truly looking for resolution then you must alter your ability to decipher the difference between what is destroying our nation and what is simply taunting our preconceived notion of innocent behavior.

CHAPTER 11

FOREVER FRIENDS

This world has been quilted by people from all walks of life. Although our deeper instincts are susceptible to all sorts of ridicule, during this particular instance we will glide through a journey that only the closest of friends can adhere to. You see, without any question, all of the deserving folks in this society should be given the opportunity to be submerged into a sacred bond with another human being. Therefore I would like to share with an entire coalition of inhabitants how jovial it is to be in the midst of a special relationship with that one unique individual. This type of splendor can evolve with one particular friend, a beloved sibling, or even a once in a lifetime sweetheart. At any rate, the experience in its entirety is priceless, topped with a celebration of pure admiration for the true meaning of the word friend.

The most valuable relationships are amongst those which we have grown to take advantage of in our everyday lives. You certainly don't have to search the world over to find this incredible person, because you have already shared an entire lifetime of unforgettable remembrances. This extraordinary individual can share both the most exhilarating and dispiriting moments beyond that to which any other person on this planet can compare. In my illustration this person is better known as my leader in life, my greatest ally, and my wholehearted grantor of inspiration. She is my sister, and she is my friend.

I have known you for such a long time that not even the worst catastrophic episode could ever separate the bond we alone have built, strengthened, and reinforced through unconditional love. I have found a soul mate for life that only unique kindred within the same element can endure, and thus it seems rather ironic that we have our parents to thank for this resistant energy we have come to share between us. I cannot even imagine how insignificant the world may have seemed if you were not there to share in those special moments and guide me through the harsh realities of life. I will always be there to strengthen you in your greatest weakness, and from your strength I will conquer any fear. Through my successes and through my failures you have always been the light at the end of my tunnel. You have saved me from the evils of despondency, and so to you my greatest mentor, all I have to give is but a few lines from these heartfelt pages. Although words alone may never compare to my complete and sincere admiration for you, I will make every attempt to reach your inner self and find out what brings about such a miraculous sister and a lifelong friend. I shall only hope that I can someday become even half the person that you are today. To you I bestow this treasure filled with hope, encouragement, and love; for that is what you have always given to me. This is my sincere dedication to my sister, and in return we will always remain true friends that only special siblings can be.

Thus in a dissimilar instance another authentic someone will embark on the joys of friendship through the mere coincidence of life. Most of you will become familiar with this one memorable occasion by simply hearing the words "Best Friend". It takes two very exceptional people to encompass the bliss, the comfort, and even the heartache. Above and beyond it all we will endure the fortunate path fate has walked us through, and relish in harmony this fascinating connection we know as friendship.

You are the keeper of the key that belongs to my deepest and darkest secrets. When the gloom from anguish eclipsed my being, you were the hand that walked me to a brighter awakening. It is your laughter alone that I seek when I struggle to reach for a more encouraging moment than what is present. Though many of our decisions were costly, I savor every moment as if it were yesterday. No regret will I ever hold, for the friend that I have found in you is forever endearing. I can only hope that our lives will favor us through our elder years, because there is no other friend I could expect to help travel the route of ever after with. Your passion for life goes beyond the measure of my admiration and complete respect one individual could hold for another. Whatever our future holds, you will forever have a loyal companion to escort you through the bumps and bruises of life, as you have so selflessly done for me. I would like to express to you my deepest thank-you from the depths of my soul for being the best friend with whom every child, girl, and woman could hope to be blessed with.

One of the most entrancing friendships you can experience, is one that will evolve into an everlasting love. Not only can an enchanting romance be sparked from an eternal friendship, but creating a lifelong love with someone from the opposite sex or otherwise, is by far the closest you can come to the guarantee of longevity.

When you walked into my life I was already consumed by macho abomination. Thus the sweet words you whispered rekindled my desire for true love and affection. Although the adventure we chose at times seemed rather hopeless, we grasped for the strength within ourselves and created an energy so determined that nothing could hinder such a force. We ripened from that moment on and united as one bond that could conquer any obstacle, as long as we accepted the challenge and defined it through harmony. My devotion to the life we have created for ourselves was developed out of a special friendship, and from this day until the very end, our sacred intimacy will guide us into a place that very few couples are able to enjoy together. This is to my companion whom I embrace as my friend and to my darling who has spoiled with the essence of forever love. May our lives always be filled with the meaning of each other.

The miracle that people can encourage is the reward of a genuine friendship. We must enjoy the lives we create for ourselves, and honor the friendships we build with one another. There is nothing on this earth more valuable than compassion and intimacy which can be forever momentous on this bicycle ride through life. If you are the type of character who takes for granted the dedication and honesty a friend can provide, then I can only caution you that your route will end with bitterness. The loss of a friend over deceitful mischief is in itself a sad display of human ignorance. You must cherish the fraternity that defines your existence, because life doesn't support eternity as fate doesn't support predictions. Embrace the jewels that you have been given so that each day can be marked by a wondrous fortune. For those of you with a place reserved on my heart, I love you forever, and may you always be embraced by the warmth of one another.

CHAPTER 12

GARBAGE 101

I am going to teeter on the edge of the platform that links useless humanity to virtual intelligence, so hang on because subtlety will not be an aspect of this topic of conversation. This theme that will appear to be overly dissected should simply exist as a matter of common sense. However, due to its insignificance this merely guides our attention into the trivial world of manmade idiocies. In any case, as a point must always be introduced, I am referring to the trash, the trash receptacle, and the universal confusion that prevents the uniting of the two. Thus we must commemorate this occasion and the people within by presenting a text of unforgettable notoriety, thus entitling those who are responsible as the one and only Corporate Trashholes. That is correct, ladies and gentlemen, I am devoting a few simple words and a couple of pages to the keeper of trash and the contents within, because apparently there seems to be an infinite number of folks who fancy this ravishing land as an enormous, God-given, hole in the ground, made for the simple purpose of holding as much waste as humanly possible in one lifetime. If this sounds even remotely familiar then consider yourself a litter junky, and this is a special tribute with honorable mention.

The dialect in which I have chosen to desensitize may at first seem wounding, but attempt to prove yourselves worthy by maintaining an attention span long enough to grasp the concept of at least one paragraph. Inside your automobile at arms length is a rather obvious compartment designed specifically for the purpose of extinguishing those little filters attached to a smoldering hot ash. Allow me the great pleasure of specifying my viewpoint in easy to follow laymen's terms. In case that your brain has already dozed off into la la land and you're more confused than not, I am simply referring to the ashtray. Hey, whether you smoke or not is a freedom of choice which I dispense to you all of the power in the world. However, I am completely baffled by your lack of knowledge and mechanics in regards to that convenient hole in the dashboard that I mentioned earlier. If you need to discard your cigarette, then employ the resources that were devised for that purpose.

Although, there always seems to be one cigarette litter junky that can top the next. For example, there are those of you who have mastered the concept of an ashtray, but ingeniously decide to empty the container of butts on the ground or in the parking lot of a business establishment. Guess what, sherlock half-wit, somebody will now have to spend their valuable time cleaning up after your hoggish act. I know this piece of information first hand, because I along with countless other hard workers have spent a tour of time accomplishing this nonsense. If you are that anxious to dispose of a brimful of cigarettes then wait until you get home. This way you can empty the tray on your own property, and perform a festive happy dance until the whole pile mysteriously disintegrates. The clue for the day is that this miracle of events wont take place for years to come, so save yourself the added embarrassment and impractical use of energy.

Now, please allow me a moment to address the masters of rubbish who have decided that overall littering is the next best thing to perpetual laziness. First and foremost, let me declare how completely unacquainted with the use of common sense you appear to be. The only bad habit that ranks lower on the scum scale than people who burden society with the illogical use of ashtray application, are the rest of you who have successfully graduated from littering 101. You have earned your degree based on your stupendous ability to incorporate into that single brain cell the image of "let it land where it may". Bravo, not only does your apparent illiteracy come through a virtually empty skull, but now you're on the expressway to creating a junkyard haven for this beautiful planet earth. Congratulations, I can only hope that life will present you with the same courtesy that you have so freely dispensed onto the rest of your domain. However, before I exit this paragraph I would like nothing more than for you to accept my donation of unwanted advice. I cannot judge you for your personal cleanliness (although I may), and how you maintain your personal lifestyle on your personal property. However, you have no right designating a trash can out of any place you see fit. Therefore I would like to take you on a free ride into the world of trash can hospice, so that you can comply with standard regulations of the hidden secret garbage law. You see, there are these fabulous bins that emanate in an array of various shapes and sizes. Inside these special bins you will find a plastic bag which serves the purpose of storing all sorts of garbage. In public establishments the words TRASH RECEPTACLE will be imprinted on the front of these bins in big, bold, lettering. These distinctive words will allow you to proceed putting your trash inside the bin, on top of the other waste. Stay with me, because the key words in the previous sentence were, inside the bin; not outside, not beside, not on top, but inside. Of my own free will I have chosen to run-through the issue using very simple words so that everyone intellectually upgraded or otherwise will comprehend.

I am now under the distinct impression that spreading around mutual respect for each other, along with honoring the grounds of this earth, have become equivalent to the prevention of sharing STD's. I certainly don't get a provocative hidden pleasure from picking up after some cretin who has been infected by habitual laziness, and evidently perceives themselves as being so lily-white that they are above walking over to the trash can and disposing of a piece of garbage. Wake up folks, because this country is not referred to as the land of the free so that people can become liberated to make the ground one adjoining land fill after another. We are speaking of something so effortless that a two-year-old could understand the concept. Realistically I'm not trying to encourage people to run out and perform brain surgery. This is simply not a matter that we can continue to neglect because we are too engrossed in self-preoccupation to be burdened by the idea of disposing properly. Endeavor the possibility of conquering 0° - 110° weather merely to pick up trash from the ground that you didn't fling there in the first place.

Listen here trashholes, you have no excuse for being compulsive litterbugs, so incorporate the meaning of responsibility into your cluttered lifestyles. Otherwise do us all a favor by renting a tiny space in the most remote corner of the world and have a round-the-clock litter party announcing VIP litter junkies exclusively. Please feel free to remain there for eternity unless you suddenly become attacked by a tribe of environmentalists who will beat you into clear conscience submission. Remember, boys and girls, littering is a crime and when you've contacted oblivion you will be fined.

CHAPTER 13

CASUALTY OF PAIN

I have chosen to approach a very sobering issue that is taking place in our society more so than we would like to admit. I will be addressing a specific collection of females who are submerged into a world of reclusion, secured by denial, and the monstrosity that will imprison them at any cost. To every aching soul I will appeal, thus praying for a difference to be felt in the heart of at least one dying spirit. This forsaken universe is confusing our own belief of pure harmony only to place a veil over the face of an unspoken fear. Thus I must oblige this responsibility, and shed a glimmer of light on a neglected injustice that ordinarily transpires behind closed doors. In any case, I would like to concern my efforts towards the mournfulness associated with domestic violence and the hope beyond a life of sheer terror. Although I am aware of the efforts brought forth by the operation of nonprofit organizations who specialize in this particular field, I believe there is a tremendous rupture between finding the inner courage to remove yourself from the clutches of a violent atmosphere, and obtaining the help that is ultimately crucial for survival. My goal is to reach into the aching soul of a dispirited woman, and rekindle the spark which lights the torch between the vanished courage and the extinct animation that became entombed within so long ago. I will also take a few moments to examine the invincible male who solely exists for the mere purpose of complete domination, along with coercive mind control, and physical mastery over a frail being. As my words fall onto these pages, I must come to the realization that I may never have the opportunity to reach the hearts of those who suffer, because of those who inflict pain. Yet if I can miraculously convince even one deserving female to leave the clutches of her strangulating partner, then my goal will have superceded my own expectations which are surrounded by the doubt of an unlikely transformation.

The meaning of love may be perceived in many fashions. However, as a victim of abuse you have been brainwashed to idealize a completely false sense of the word, and denied the opportunity to have an encounter with the authentic love that lies beyond the misinterpretation you have come to know. Your imposter to the prince charming world portrays himself as an absolute gentlemen with the pure qualities that are genuinely unparalleled to his male counterparts. However, deep within his coloring, lies a Jeckle and Hyde personality that is fueled by anger and violent tendencies. After he slowly conforms your mind into an acute dependency, his ulterior demons begin to surface. Now you have succumbed to a plight where your self-esteem is in the hands of a poisonous dictator, and your is life determined by his desire for ruthless supremacy. When he believes you have not reached his expectations, he's immediately enraged and feels provoked enough to release his pent up anger in the form of a close-fisted blow to the first part of your body he can make contact with. You love him enough to hold in your heart and mind that he will eventually transform into the magnificent creature you once knew. However, you must come to the realize that his mind is diluted by so much anger, inevitably he will become his own fueling destruction. The possibility for total self resurrection can only be made possible followed by his acceptance that a destructive behavior is the root of his mental demise.

Before I waste my time addressing the grisly lurch who inflicts horrific pain on a delicate soul, I must first utilize my time productively by speaking with the victim of unconditional agony.

Every thought you have must be exhausted by the feeling of never-ending days that are perpetually corrupted by fear. He has deluded your idea of a perfect, happily ever life, with the image of personal blame for the collapse of an ideal marriage. Please abstain from what you perceive to be a rational thought, and take my plea for your overall well being to a far better lifestyle that is created by the security of peace. Without any question you are an astonishing human being who is surrounded by a world that is pleading with your heart to unlock the door to your undiscovered compassion. Although I am not acquainted with you on a more intimate level, I recognize that you reserve within your soul something so glorious that you believe to be empowered enough to change the ways of a fearsome partner. You must locate your inner strength and combine this with the energy you have exerted towards this pseudo-caring leach, and free yourself from his Alcatraz style environment. Fear nothing from his pursuit, for you can easily become lost in the clutter of this mass world. You are petrified of this hunter and understandably so, but now it is essential for you to transform all of your fright into raw courage. Your body is only a shell for your outer being, it is not a burial ground for your spirit and soul. One ounce of strength is enough to lead you on the yellow brick road where independence will welcome you with open arms. When you finally make the decision to abandon this foreign self, you will be introduced to a miraculous human being that has been buried within. Through a tour of soul searching, you will become the liberated and independent woman that you were always meant to be. Thus you will learn that the only inhabitant in life you can possibly change for better or for worse, is the person who is looking back at you when you look in the mirror. Your past shall become a former obstacle that presents a promising and prosperous future. Though your first step may seem like a giant and unattainable hurdle right now, you can obtain this liberation, but first you must believe in yourself.

This is to the master of domination who is obviously suffering from self worth deficiency syndrome (SWDS). Apparently you have created your own stature in life while lacking in every area of success offered to a human being. Since failure is your weak link, authority over a female is your last chance at desperately accomplishing what you deem as greatness in your pathetic existence. Yes, unfortunately I must sink to your level so that we can relate. You have literally mind raped another human being of their dignity and value only to glorify a fragment of usefulness that is defective in the day to day ritual you justify as a lifestyle. You're a barbaric numskull that ranks lower than saturated cow feces, and apparently you have just recently discovered your last functioning brain cell; which happens to be grossly impaired. Since you've become aware of the fact that you are a waste of space, you have taken this mind shattering awakening and used it as a tool to break down the minds of those you deem as being the weaker species. You have succumbed to this ludicrous notion that total control over your partner will instill an overwhelming fear that will prevent her from ever leaving your wrath. You are living with deluding paranoia, so every decision you conjure up is ruled by your own insecurities. Through predomination over your mate, you compensate for your spineless actions that contribute to violence and overall abuse. However, allow me to enlighten your chauvinistic viewpoint. Every person has a breaking point, especially a woman of physical and/or mental abuse. When the time comes, and your spouse reaches this threshold, you may very well find yourself flying solo or habituating in hellfire eternity. At this point in your meager life you hardly deserve companionship, which happens to be a treasure presented by the joys of life. Only those who thrive on respect should be pampered by fate, and the rest of you can test your endurance with an unpleasant journey into eternity. How dare you venture into falsehood only to presume that your life is any more superior than that of your partner. If a haunting past is driving you into an uncontrollable fit of rage, then quest for closure through therapy, cease your violence on the blameless. Masterminding your chosen escort in life may end your state of being in a more vicious way than the discipline you are inflicting on the one you allegedly dote on. Punishment is served in many forces, thus allowing you the opportunity to realize that your actions today may be the evidence which convicts you tomorrow. Although my words may appear insignificant because of my female status, let it not be left unsaid that you have been forewarned. I am a determined woman who thrives on the potency of estrogen, and when your victims of abuse prosper using the same hormonal strength, you will drown in your very own pool of weakness and self-pity.

A few pages in this book may never touch the lives of those who are in dire need, but it is mandatory to intervene at some point. For those of you who do not suffer at the hands of a domestic violent abuser, lecture with my words or use your very own, but fight for those who cannot find the courage to resist the sovereignty of their narcotic, Hitler-type, husbands. Imagine rendering your entire life to the fear of abuse, and spending every day wondering how much terror each minute will have in store for you. This is not an effortless situation that offers a quick fix solution, but to turn a blind eye is just as cruel as the abuse in itself. If your friend or loved one dies at the hands of maltreatment, would your conscience be guilty of neglect? If you are a casualty in the domestic violence war then allow yourself the reward of life, because you were not born to this earth for the purpose of suffering at the hands of another. From this standpoint taking action is so much easier to vocalize than to accomplish. However, if we conjoin on a moral high ground, then we may be able to rescue the victim from that one fatal incident. This is not supposed to be considered a norm for such a charitable society, so instead of tail tucking let's put the pressure on the criminal who puts his hands on the spouse.

CHAPTER 14

GET THE LOAD OUT OF IT

It would appear during this day and age, through over active schedules and generally hectic lifestyles, that society as a whole has made a colossal attempt to conform in a manner which offers to meet our everyday demands. For example, through the flare of technology the automatic teller machines have prevailed to satisfy the consumer who has declined to endure the more personal affects associated with face to face banking. Aside from personal security this advancement in electronics also offers an efficient and more rapid response time to your banking needs. Alongside modern banking, our local supermarkets have also blessed us with the convenience of rapidity by securing a few specific aisles with the word express lane attached to a bright neon sign. With an overabundance of glaring obviousness, these checkout lanes were designed to assure that the one stop shopper could exit the grocery store as quickly as he came in. In any case, these systematic amenities have been structured to bring ease to the consumer, and less stress to society as an entirety. However, this brings me to question those who belligerently abuse the comfort and briskness associated with these economically correct facilities. Then after I incriminate those who have negligently inconvenienced our accessibility to a timesaving lifestyle, I would like to dwell on one last minute sucking dilemma. The issue that must be addressed is the concept behind the infamous waiting room. It seems that a patient's valued time is becoming less important compared to the idea of creating an assembly line of people in order to collect a pocket full of greenbacks. Basically during this segment I will be breaking down the barriers between thrifty time application versus deterioration of the entire notion. Once again I am merely trying to instigate systematic relief to an environment that is destined for chaos.

First and foremost, I would like to point out that the ATM was designed for an entire population longing for mere simplicity along with total convenience. Thus it is irritating to sit in line behind some anal retentive nincompoop who feels the need to transact every payment, deposit, and withdrawal for an entire month's worth of living. Now I do acknowledge that all of these features are accessible to you, however, an ounce of common courtesy for your fellow banking members really demonstrates an act of raw intelligence. I'm only pointing this out for one minor reason. When rush hour traffic is in the midst of a jam from an entourage of vehicles lined up behind you, that are now backed up onto the road, it's time to reconsider the logic you have incorporated into your forty-five minute transaction. Please don't misinterpret my blatant bitchiness, because unfortunately I do realize that you possess just as many rights to the ATM as the other seething patrons behind you. However, it seems that common sense would allow you to reason with the fact that all of your banking affairs are not required to be processed at the exact same time. Maybe just for the sake of variation you might try breaking your visits down into five minute or less intervals, thus allowing you to distribute equal time to the rest of the electronic banking members. Feel the power, it's all in your hands now. However, if you are in the middle of some self-involved ego trip that penetrates feelings of ungenerous behavior, then I can only wish upon you a bout with the same detainment you have so graciously inflicted upon others. Last but not least, I bear a great deal of optimism that your ATM card will eventually become swallowed by the wrath of the machine, because even technology spares little tolerance for obsessive compulsive, deliberately obtrusive disorder. Try to retain in your pea brain the words *advanced technology*, because they do symbolize a certain degree of defining velocity for a reason.

Now I must scurry on to another ruffling of the feathers dilemma. Envision for a brief moment that you have just arrived at the supermarket for the simple purpose of buying a few odds and ends. After conquering an exhausting day, you don't expect that you will have to wait in line for the same amount of time it would take to get on the water slide during a holiday weekend at Willie World. This should prove to be true, especially if you are standing behind a pair of courteous patrons who are respectfully abiding by the eight items or less sign that is distinctly posted, in visible view, directly above the chipper cashier who was smiling not even five minutes ago. However, as you are heading towards the aisle marked express lane, a total freak of nature whips in front of you pushing a cart that is brimming with groceries. How can this be? I don't see him sporting around dark glasses while being guided by a seeing eye dog. All of a sudden your total frame of mind has just become preoccupied by feelings of complete irritation towards a burden on society. Maybe this infantile idiot will sum up the entire experience by flashing a charge card that is clearly beyond its credit limit. Why not wait another fifteen minutes since this thick-witted cretin has already disregarded the meaning of the word express. Excuse me while I take a moment to unburden myself from these words that are wrestling to disgorge from my overactive voice box. For the sake of total logic, people who dive into this category are the reason for a complete breakdown in the entire communication process regarding fast pace. I mean, at what point exactly do you become so very confused? Is it the eight items or less sign that throws your whole thought process into a frenzied whirlwind? If it is a complex matter such as illiteracy, then you may want to consider signing up for the hooked on grocery store policy phonics program. I am sure it has proven to be very useful for many alike. On the other hand, if you are just blatantly disrespectful then please abstain from the public scene, for you are surely to be considered a menace to the rest of the shoppers who simply do not have time to deal with your weak portrayal of intellect. I am sure you can consult Mary Mary quite contrary, to find out how her garden grows. However, if you choose to bless us with your presence then abide by the procedures that allow the entire supermarket community to remain in harmony at a rapid tempo. This will prevent a discontented shopper from being taken over by a mysterious force that coerces her to remove a few useless items from your basket while your back is turned.

Finally I would like to take a quick moment to address one more pet peeve in the tardy sector. There is nothing more inflaming than having to sit in the waiting room for the length of time it would take to conceive and raise a child through graduation day. Before I begin, I must say that without any doubt we would all be gumming our food with one foot in the grave if it were not for the doctors and dentists of today. However, to our beloved medical professionals, I must declare that it is rather bedeviling that you would schedule twenty people within five minutes of one another, and possess the knowledge that each patient will be waiting for a ridiculous amount of time. Unless this is some get rich quick scheme initiated by a doctor who has decided that the easiest way to prolong business is by making a room full of sick people sit together long enough to ingest each other's germs, then you have no legitimate excuse for fooling away our time. As far as the dentists are concerned, I can't even fathom how you can rationalize a forty-five minute wait. It has become almost mandatory to clear our schedule for half of the day primarily for the time squandered waiting for your over-scheduled posteriors. I tip my hat for the heroics you bring to this plagued world, but our time is also in demand elsewhere. Let me just conclude with one last point, and direct this towards the indecisive patient. If you have enough energy to pick up the phone and schedule an appointment, then get your weary ego in the vehicle, and drive to the building where you have made the obligation to show up. All it takes is one imprudent half-wit to initiate an entire system of perpetual cancellations that will lead to a doctor's disgruntled revenge and over-scheduling madness. Otherwise concoct a home remedy, and allow the rest of the ill community to eventually obtain the care that we have been so diligently waiting to receive for over an hour and a half now. Thank you and may good health inspirit us all.

I would like to bring closure to this chapter by maintaining that our industrious society is being designed to satisfy our accelerated lifestyles. Though it may seem that all of the simpleton backwoods genius types are bombarding any aim towards advancement, we must keep in mind that every individual has a different mentality speed. This unfortunate glitch may prevent a few inhabitants from actually obtaining the necessary skills required to conventionalize. Ultimately the public atmosphere is blueprinted to herd us along like a flock of sheep, so we must work hand in hand with those who wander off into the brown covered pastures. The point is, that in an overpopulated world there is simply very little time to dawdle around like you have a boulder-size rock stuck in your underwear. Living in tempo is a decision that we as a people have elected to follow, so if you are truly unsatisfied with the outcome please send all complaints in a self-addressed envelope. Technology is the proof, so keep up with the times, or stay out of the way, but don't nuisance the rest of society with your clock-monopolizing nonsense.

CHAPTER 15

FREELOADING PARASITES

In light of a dishonorably contaminated system, I would like to present an entire chapter to the money-sucking frauds that are festering within the realms of our society. Allow me to preoccupy your minds for a moment, devoting your attention towards an economically diseased ailment that has been plaguing our nation far too long. The issue that I shall dwell upon is the welfare system and the leeches that are preying on the holes within. This segment will be dissected into two primary categories. The first breed that I will focus on are the baby factory families who have literally made a career out of unprotected sex and child bearing. Next I will envision the logic behind authorizing food stamps and free currency to the obviously capable laborer of welfare manipulation. Finally, I would like to summarize the injustice by quenching your appetite with a full serving of welfare de jour, and the authentic ingredients that notarized its original intent. I deem it necessary to conclude this introduction by declaring that any soft spot I may tap dance on can clearly be strengthened with a little motivation displayed in the form of an exertion ritual. I will also try to remain within the realms of the back wood variety dialect, so you don't have to be burdened with the chore of fetching after the dictionary. Thus you are not required to leave the warm imprint which has taken on the shape of your body, and has now become a permanent outline on the sofa cushions.

How very numbing it is to see your parade of children flocking around the grocery store in a most uncivilized manner. While you are thumbing through this week's variety of colorless food stamps, maybe you could take a moment to tame these wildly out of control little people who are performing the role of bratty child on sugar high. What a coincidence it is that you have the same number of children as you do grocery bags, and a spectacular array of brand name food products to satisfy each and every one in your collection of neonates. I certainly don't mean to present myself with an old-maidish type of demeanor, because I do acknowledge that these children are not to blame for their parent's blemished version of reality. However, as one who chooses not to procreate at this point in time, it seems I am forking out a great deal of money every single payday to help aid your army of perpetual surprises. Can you see the bottom of my cart? Of course you can, but don't let that burden your mind with guilt because I am thrilled to be buying your overactive rugrats a seven course meal through taxes pillaged from my paycheck every single week. I will be thinking of you blissfully as I am munching on my peanut butter and crackers while washing it down with generic soda pop. I am not going to solely reprimand you for this utter humiliation that is consuming our society. If welfare was less accessible and less rewarding based on the number of children you bore, then possibly you would be more apt to indulge in labor that pays versus pains. It seems more reliable to relinquish your monthly state checks towards providing you with free daycare instead of continually punishing the American workers for your uninterrupted pregnancies. This lack of free income might inspire you to get off your job-free derriere and join the rest of the employed community. At least then you would be giving back to the jackpot that you so freely indulge in. I am completely fed up with the reckless concept that supports a multitude of families who do not comprehend the physics behind rubber raincoats. Especially since there are several alternative means for you to purchase various assortments at a relatively dirt cheap cost. Not to mention how inexpensive the cost is compared the impulsive behavior which led you to an aftermath that practically out numbers Jerry Lewis. The moral of the story is, get off your ill-bred buttocks, locate a job that does not involve mattress aerobics, and take responsibility for your umpteen number of kids, or don't bring them forth for others to finance.

Now that I have proclaimed an indefinite cease fire on the perpetual aphrodisiacs, I would like to dispense a few words on all of the leeches who are able to terminate welfare, but continue to exhaust the system with their bloodsucking fraudulent existence. Not only do I nearly burst into flames imagining the buffoon that has successfully blind-sided the system, but now I am truly baffled by the obvious breeches within the welfare community that are apparently being ignored or highly disregarded. Allow me to display my irritation in a nonchalant manner. Yeah right! I am referring to all of the freeloaders who have managed to find employment (better known as the American dream), yet through a second income known as welfare they are basking in a luxurious lifestyle. These pretentious swindlers are sporting around in high priced automobiles along with wallowing in the comforts of a lavish home. I would like these American imposters to choke on a few of my words. Although your pseudo lifestyle appears similar to those who actually work hard for there riches, eventually your covert operation will surface as deception for which you should be permanently branded with the letter F upon capture. This way each and every American worker can identify all of the community slugs which are now bought and paid for. You see, what appears to be lacking in your vocabulary are the words guilt and utter humiliation. Obviously you are truly burdened with, I don't know, let's say maybe mmmhh...PRIDE!! On the other hand, since you have not educated yourself with any sort of moral standard, possibly you may want consider a lesson in self worth and dignity. How dare you force those who productively labor into a state of ration because you're openly raping them of there gross paychecks. Snooze time is over Uncle Sam because there is an over-abundance of conspiracy festering around the system which was designed to support those who are truly in need. Keep in mind cretin, that redemption strikes in many forms, and every capital offender has his day.

We are truly being taken advantage of by the lack of action that would eliminate welfare almost entirely. I wouldn't be so disgusted by the mockery if the money wasn't being seized right from our own back pockets while are hands are completely tied. Many of us are struggling to make ends meet while others are floating by us on the cloud with the greenback and silver lining. I will not contest that some folks should be able to employ the true purpose of welfare, however, unless you're handicapped, disabled, or you need a very temporary boost back on your feet, you have no prerogative even looking at the welfare office. I could care less how many kids you're parading around, because that was a matter of choice. The last time I checked, a female's womb can only incubate through one means, and it's certainly not from the miracle of immaculate conception. If the government wants to continue to indulge in anal exploitation, then so be it, but don't volunteer the rest of the nation for mandatory ankle grabbing. Basically what it comes down to is that these folks are acting as hemorrhoids, and instead of finding a cure we would rather lubricate the problem for temporary relief.

My real purpose here is not to advertise for Preparation H, but to shed a light on an injustice that is literally robbing the country, and generously giving to those who don't deserve a dime. Welfare should not be a bonus for illogical actions. Instead it should act as a strict stepping stone for those who need a helping hand. Consequences need to be enforced for those who participate in negligent intercourse. I am not proposing that sex should be a criminal act, because it is a personal choice that every person has the right to make. However, welfare has become a crutch for those who engage in actions that they choose not to take responsibility for nine months down the road. The children are the true victims of this shame, and they are being exposed to a lifestyle which is unfit for even those who choose to live in disgust. If you cannot provide for a child then don't bear one, because we cannot afford them either. If you are working and receiving welfare then you deserve to be severely penalized upon admission of guilt. Poverty isn't a crime, dishonesty is a shame, but welfare is negligence of the two combined which should be an offense in itself.

CHAPTER 16

TAKE THIS SCALE AND SHOVE IT

The mirror and the scale, despite the fact that they are both inanimate objects that bridge the gap between physical weight and eye capturing beauty, have literally become one of our worst enemies in regards towards personal vanity. Our mental function does not permit one's self to solely capture the beauty of the embodied silhouette, and inevitably our time is spent discerning then concealing our authentic imperfections. I am not proclaiming that every human creature in society looks in the mirror only to expect an image of repulsion, however, we have limited our ideas of natural freedom simply to become accepted in a society that only sees what our eyes will tangibly permit. We have become so diluted into thinking that a mass of flesh and muscles, held in strength by bones, will ultimately dictate our status in the minds of the fastidiously selective, that a person cannot be entirely embraced at any shape, size, or physical flaw that accompanies their inner package. We have truly fooled ourselves into achieving a flawless visage, merely for the purpose of satisfying the superficial attitude that feeds into an over-commercialized industry; openly welcome by our society. Instead of dwelling on thick, thin, or otherwise, I am going to take a more in-depth look at a cruel environment, represented by all discriminating trends, that is virtually destroying our ability to embrace the spirit and uniqueness one has to offer. Although I believe a majority of the fashion industry preys on the delicate perception outlining our hope of acceptance and poisons our logic, I must also point out that our weak resistance only feeds the monster who is injecting this prejudice.

The fact of the matter is that the average American is hardly carrying the figure of the waif models that are exploited throughout the commercial and fashion industry. In light of this newfound hypocrisy I am left completely bewildered about why we allow this false portrayal of proportions to influence our keen sense of perception for the latest fad. With all due respect to this uncomprehending industry, I feel the need to introduce them to the planet earth where the women are built curvaceous and the men sport around as robust. I am a little baffled at where you extracted this bean pole look from, but if I were you I would demand an immediate refund for the purchase of decomposed seeds. Obviously you are trying to feed us a look that simply does not exist for the average person, (unless of course we were all still basking in the luxury of eighth grade swimwear while expelling any form of puberty). Yet you still thrive financially because of our own lack of acknowledgement. Without our greenbacks this flourishing industry of falsehood would no longer exist, and so the question still remains. Why is this phony industry that is run by distorted imagery prospering with our money? What it basically boils down to is that we are shrouding our true self image by continuing to close our eyes, thus voluntarily authorizing a false representation of our society.

Let us resolve the issue by stating that the fashion gurus can choke on their own hypocrisies, while the human culture can obtain enough backbone to help suffocate the deterioration of our true being. Realistically it doesn't matter how much of this fashion infidelity we're spoon fed, it is that we're too mind impotent to escape the transparent message. Instead, we should be overwhelming this esteem-sucking industry by employing a universal attitude that promotes an in-depth look at the spiritual beauty within. Maybe we could obtain the goal of uniting on a common ground where outer appearance is excluded from the interference of pure virtue. I refuse to believe we have been so ensnared by commercialized brainwash, that our whole sense of rationale has been entirely depleted. However, before we can conquer the false exploitation of the human body, we must initiate a universal alteration of how we visually and physically dissect one another.

It is very sobering to know that we support a demeaning and perpetual lack of self esteem, which nobody dares to admit for fear that we might actually accept each other for inner beauty versus degrading one another for outer appearance. Yet isn't it rather hypocritical how we all pretend to embrace an attitude of acceptance, until a person of excessive weight, underweight, or any other so-called abnormality, walks into a room of self-proclaimed perfectionists. This is when the crudest remarks prevail, which of course follow shortly after the snickering subsides. Everyone is prone to the defiance of harassment and to carry the name of the heckler, regardless of how determined you are to live in denial. At what point in life did we become so tainted by superficiality that our approval in society is determined by the appearance of our bodies? We have become this way because we are lacking a certain amount of crisis in our lives that would force upon us desperately the need to survive. Should we all become ravished of our own greedy lifestyles, while being forced to behoove the detriment that is starving some third world countries, I am afraid our nation would become extinct versus fighting to live. We are not burdened with the hassle of critical survival issues, because we are not faced by them. The issues of detrimental crisis we do encounter are brought upon by our own willingness to ignore the obvious. I doubt the people in Ethiopia give a rats ding-dong what the latest trend is, they just want to eat. Again my point is toward focusing on this issue alone, and not to incorporate a whole rash of travesties that we do endure.

My view on this subject is only supported by the obviousness that we cannot cry victim for something that we virtually bring upon ourselves. If the outer self is the only entity that you're willing to embrace, then it is quite crystal clear this is the only thing you will ever see. This country would not be comprised of such a vast amount people who are struggling with their true identity if there wasn't always someone standing in the shadow waiting to prey on their insecurities. Whether you're fat, thin, black, white, handicapped, or a mixture of your own unique distinctions, I will continue to say that we all face our own society deemed shortcomings by striving to surpass our own self critiquing, and we should be given the opportunity to do so without belittlement from others. Do not continue to be a victim to the foolishness by feeding into this unrealistic portrayal of the average person. We are given so little time here on earth to bask in the luxury of life, and obsessing over physical appearance is a very dispirited way to ration your time. I propose that we should do away with all of the scales and the mirrors that are corroding our ideals of natural beauty. We would be forced to admire each other before the mask is painted on. Could we take off the blinders and still love, or must we always fit into this mold of false perfection?

CHAPTER 17

THE NEW KKK - KIDS KILLING KIDS

As the course of time embraces each day, it is escorted by a chill in the air brought upon by previous tragic events. The once-upon-a-time idea which suggested that only third world countries endure the shame of their own civilians declaring war against the innocent, is a historical image of our past. Unfortunately, as the horrifying issues of the days unfold, it is our nation that wreaks havoc on their own free land and the people that inhabit these grounds. The future of this country will be entrusted into the hands of our children, and when a remote percentage declare a state of execution on their own peers, it is absolutely frightening to envision what the hereafter will have in store for our people. Over the last few years we have come to witness a devastating eruption of venomous behavior overpowering the morale of the young. This act of violence has instilled a mind-controlling fear that brings us to wonder when the next school mass murder will strike upon the innocents of our society. Through my words I am guiding you into a mournful topic that must be addressed time and again until the tolerance of violent corruption is washed away from the lives of those who have already eliminated the value of humanity from their blackened souls.

When a child is capable of murder we tend to distribute the blame amongst a wide variety of influential factors. These varying elements may include the parents, the schools, and a conglomeration of outside potencies; all which could potentially corrupt the mind of any desperate juvenile. Many children are not natural-born killers, so this will only persuade one's curiosity to question which of life's instances corroded the molding of this young mind. I will not declare that every professionally developed option I am about to analyze is the answer behind this tragic outbreak of horrific events. I do not claim to bear any sort of degree which would permit me to give a sociological solution to this topic.

I am simply a member of this society who often wonders about the mind set of our youth. At what point do these children decide that it is acceptable to seek their own justice in such a brutal manner?

When a child is miraculously born into this world, the mother and father instantaneously begin to mold and influence the infant's mind. As the following years succumb to the endless tutoring through a parent's vicariously-taught unconditional love, a remarkable human being develops. Through these first few precious years the overall intervention of his forbearers plays a vital role on his perception of life thus far, which ultimately factors into an identity. Keeping that in mind opens a whole new inquiry on the radical upbringing one must have sustained in order to ultimately achieve such unconscionable behavior. I myself have not embarked on the mystery of parenting, thus in the eyes of most, this lack of experience prohibits me from placing any sort of judgement on the creators of a juvenile mass murderer. Regardless of my inexperience I have still come to the conclusion, developed through my background in existing, that it would seem as though these parents must accept some sort of responsibility for their child's distorted view of right and wrong. My assumption may only hold a smidgen of accuracy, however, it does seem rather logical considering the parents maintained the function of role model during their crucial infant and toddler years. I am having a difficult time swallowing the idea that a child can execute a massive killing spree without previously transmitting some sort of sign that divulges a pattern of unusual or reckless behavior. Secondly, how is it possible for these kids to create such a detailed plan within the comfort of their own home? Respecting your child's privacy is one thing, but giving them complete control over their own freedom seems a bit extreme. I am not ashamed to admit that if a I had to conduct a covert intelligence operation to detail every moment of my child's actions in order to prevent this from happening in the first place, than so be it. It certainly pales in comparison to the alternative that results from allowing too much personal space to begin with. However, without living in their homes, or walking a mile in their shoes, it is very difficult to play a guessing game when given so very few clues about the day to day lifestyle which reared them into such annihilating anti-social monstrosities. If the parents played the role of protector to the fullest, and tried to combat the demons that haunted the child, maybe the environment away from the home triggered the lashing out.

Aside from the parent's and the child's home life, the schools also play a vital role on governing the influential factors that shape these vulnerable minds. It doesn't appear to be a freak coincidence that all of the massacres are staged on the grounds of our youth filled learning facilities. The rage is always focused on the enemy within, and yet through intense chaperoning all of these childhood malfunctions are minimized into some teenage hormonal category. We are all defined by our own characteristics, but it time to become educated on the difference between a self-proclaimed individual and a disturbed outcast. Through policies and strict regulations the schools are assuming that the administration has a tight grip on any resistant action that arises. However, as the times are abruptly changing for the absolute worst, the kids are prematurely slipping away. They are relying on one another for guidance, but this type of direction has been significantly tainted by the vast corruption dominating our society. In light of this information we must now make a decision that will significantly change the traditional role of the schools overall functions. This substantial modification will affect everyone from the outcasts to the scholarly. Through intense deliberation of outweighing the advantages to the disadvantages, we must conclude whether or not we shall turn our schools into a once again safe haven through the use of advanced security measures. By installing security cameras, metal detectors, and upgrading the idea of hall monitor by replacing them with security guards, many folks will deem this as declaring a miniature version of martial law, while revising the current name of schools to prisons. On the other hand, almost everywhere you go this same form of action is being institutionalized in a similar manner. We are basically permitting security throughout the entire nation, yet when it is required of our school systems to enforce a higher degree of safety, we would rather strike up an irrational controversy versus taking any measure necessary to protect the innocent. Whether you agree with this or not, all forms of precaution should be glorified in exchange for the current tail tucking that permits this open arena of childhood slaughter. This may not be the answer that will cure the hatred in the minds of our young, but it is a realistic start at protecting the lives of the children. We cannot allow for them to declare themselves the next endangered species.

As technology leaps into unimaginable greatness, we must also determine how much of it is necessary in the aiding of our survival, and decide whether or not this enhancement bridges the gap between life and manmade inevitable dissolution. The computer, which was ultimately thought of as a miracle for its ability to act as our second brain, has now become the endless information central support system for both the ordinary folk and the psychotic demon folk. Through the infamous internet, certain freaks of nature have found a government-free safe haven to exploit their demented version of reality, while giving little regard to the potentially destructive force behind that one dot.com. Here is a perfect example of a devise that had the possibility of bringing an enormous amount of intellectual wealth to our society. Unfortunately, it has now become the link to a vast amount of dangerous variety that is distorting the minds of our future. At some point in time regulations will have to be enforced to weed out all of the injurious non intellectual information from the positively enlightening data. Of course, this will instigate furious behavior from a whole rash of enraged mortals who will self-righteously bawl about the vivid tap dance that is being performed on their first amendment rights. However, just as you are not permitted to walk into a crowded movie theatre and yell " FIRE", you should not be allowed to openly glorify human slaughter to anyone you see fit. Yes, you should be able to express your opinion regardless of the brutality involved in your twisted rationale, but it should become mandatory that a barrier is placed between that colorless information and the free will of our children to discover it. Hooray for them when they embark upon adulthood where they can decide for themselves which path they choose to follow, but until then we as the experienced mentors are still responsible for the physical and mental well being of our young.

We who bear the intellect and maturity that faculties adulthood, can distinguish the difference between shock rock and a Satanist who is deliberately trying to poison one's inner soul. Listening to an artist's lyrics and overanalyzing them to the point of creating a diversion through protest is the only solution we have chosen to contribute, rather than discovering the true meaning behind each verse. Therefore, this ill-conceived music is the forbidden candy jar in the eyes of the children, simply because it is an adult-perceived outrage of corruptive brainwash. Of course they will run to what they are told is prohibited, just the same as we all did during our teen years. Although shock rock has been around since the beginning of time, the difference now is how the entire idea has surpassed the boundary that supports rationale and reason. Combine the forbidden, depression, low self esteem, lack of a supportive environment, and top it off with misinterpreted lyrics, of course you will have a disaster waiting to happen. If a forest fire is out of control, you cannot blame the trees for their coincidental part in the destruction, you have to start with the arsonist. Prevention and intervention are the only things that will stop this madness, and this is the responsibility of both the mentors and the creators. If musicians are conveying a message marked by the demons that haunt their own pasts, it would be even more empowering for them to positively inspire and strengthen those kids who are experiencing this same type of misfortune. Until then, we as the adults must take the time to educate ourselves with the message behind dark music, so we can interpret the true meaning to our children. They are going to listen to it regardless of what you say, so wouldn't it be better if they understood the lyrics from a point of view that is more realistic than the message they will derive themselves.

Another way to receive national recognition while embracing the control of world-wide pause, is to enforce an act of such brutality that life itself is engulfed in a near standstill. Our link to the dysfunctional world is on display right in our own living rooms. The devastation brought directly to our lives through the means of headline news has literally become an immunity to our minds, because every occurrence is simply another typical everyday happening that we've learned to accept as part of our existence. In the here and now it seems that the most volatility brutal acts receive extraordinary recognition, and the fact remains that any portrayal of human retaliation is exploited through the media. This world wide acknowledgement is now becoming a lure for our youth and an invitation to successfully execute any lethal plot. I am not proclaiming that the media has glorified these acts of childhood slayings, however, it seems like the idea of excelling in the midst of worldwide attention, through enacting bitter vengeance, is a temptation for any antisocial and depressed child. We must agree that this holds especially true for the kids who are rejected by their immediate peers. The minds of our young are being tainted by a gross amount of deranged information while being spoon fed all the poisoned morals of a few demented students. Although it is the responsibility of the media to report all kinds of news, they should be spending an greater amount of that time focusing on the kids who are making a positive impact on the world today, instead of volunteering so much time on the actions empowered by hatred.

In order to summarize this topic, I feel I must sacrifice one last paragraph to the innocence lost and the trust that may never have the opportunity to be regained. Thus, the fear of trusting again may strike upon our minds horrific thoughts of useless massacre. The only safe haven for our youth will be a self imposed wall which they can hide behind. We cannot allow malicious hatred to force our kids into reclusion. In order to prevent this loss of pure virtue from occurring time and again, we should cease expending all of our time distributing the blame. Dispensing in its place should be, at minimum, an equal amount of time towards strengthening the minds of the children to combat the destructive forces empowering the world, while forfeiting the idea of embracing such unconscionable behavior. School ground killing sprees are becoming a trend in our small town communities, and this act of humane destruction should have been contained after the very first onset of youth-deranged fury. How many potentially gifted humanitarians must be sacrificed to the hands of death before any tangible ideas of resolution are set into motion? We have been attacked in our homes, in our automobiles, in the work place, and now the schools have succumbed to the invasion of violence. I refuse to embrace the concept that more people exist fueled by hatred than not, so as a member of the competent and sane I propose that we fight for control of a world currently dominated by a population that is weakened by evil. School massacres may be lying dormant right now, but the issues are still very much awake.

CHAPTER 18

SELF

I am endlessly envisioning the wonders that encompass this mysterious force identified as life. Thus, I begin to challenge my kismet being with a broad array of curiosities about my own existence, and I often question whether or not my appearance on this venture was meant to bring forth a great opportunity that is yet to be discovered. During this unearthing of my true self, I often query the feelings that I harbor in my own mind towards life when it is in the fullest moment of its glory, the world that has captured my fate, and my personal battles which are both self induced and out of my control. Are these thoughts and emotions, which are endlessly animating themselves in my vivid imagination, a path that is leading me to a unique sense of my own being, or is this all just another part of the intricacy that escorts life? I am still so very much a part the youth that will eventually vanish when a person embarks upon the maturity outlined in adulthood, but the prior years seemed to have passed so very quickly, drawing me closer each day to the dawn of eternity. The world is an open hand to a vast amount of unimaginable beauty, which I hope to capture on this exotic walk escorted by my future, yet I struggle with all that is to be accomplished in my envisioned quest brought upon by my dreams. My self proclaimed promise is to achieve, at minimum, one extraordinary feat per year that will surpass the prior goals of my creation. Thus I shall suffocate regret from burdening my elder years by not submitting to a sense of ill-conceived misfortune. This is a deed that is to proclaim the most unusual of all fantasies, and a boundary worth grasping in order to exceed all limitations of defiance. Although I have already fulfilled many of my desires, I continually succumb to the worst feeling that presents itself in the form of boredom. I am truly baffled by the complexity of this sensation that I am plagued with, and I often wonder if I will ever reach the point of pure satisfaction, or will I always have this hunger that begs for more than what I have already given. Allow me to use this time to explore my inner self, thus deciding what changes I must address in order to find true happiness when the end of the road embraces me.

The ultimate goal that is first introduced to the minds of most young, is obtaining success while striving for approval in a career that is self-fulfilling. Thus far in my journey to reach the highest mountain, I have strapped myself in a standstill forced upon by my own foolish and tainted decisions. I have approached and dissected an array of what I deemed would ultimately become a fruitful calling in life, yet as each day waves good-bye, my fly by night success hitches on to the train of wasted effort. I have a purpose for my existence that I can literally feel in my bones, but I cannot bring that feeling to surface only because I have not discovered what that destined role is. I am so determined to pursue that one particular niche specifically fated in my reserve, that I may be blindsiding the obvious by searching in all the wrong places. Life is an endless and winding maze that has an obstacle to overcome at the end of each trail marked go, and every time you think you're close to reaching greatness, there sits another wall built to challenge your endurance. I have yet to locate the golden key that unlocks the door to success, but I will employ each of my failures as a stepping stone. Thus, when the time is right, I will climb to the top of the stairway that is built out of my own miscarriages, and I will do so regardless of what my peers have already envisioned for my future. Yes, I have made a tremendous amount of naïve misjudgments on this wondrous journey, but this does not qualify me as one who cannot soar above my own misfortune. In spite of it all, should I embrace the kingdom of prosperity one day, I will preserve enough righteousness to prevent losing myself in the greed of spiritual sacrifice.

Shall I ever become blessed with many a treasure, I often foresee a future that teeters on the edge of responsibility and reckless spending. If I become sightless to my own egocentricity, inevitably this uncharitable performance would lead me to a life less desirable; sparing little remorse. If I never reach the comfort zone, then it was a fantasy that was never meant to be fulfilled, and my existence will have to be compensated through another means of inner desire. What I do acknowledge is that I have already strapped myself in a financial choke hold, and if tomorrow brings with it a disastrous encounter, then I will surely be headed towards a life on the foundation of poverty. Looking back at my decisions only leads to a clouded memory, for I am unable to pinpoint the duration in which my spending became so careless. That carefree time in my life has left me in a current state of financial dehydration. I struggle to make each paycheck last until the next, and if I never make another dime I will be tied to a lasso and dragged; unable to ride the horse that carries all of my expectations. Living from one pay period to the next was certainly not in my plans, but my goals have developed immensely in comparison to what they were only a few years ago. I am determined to recover from my youthful pitfalls, because the world is not a planetary handout, and there is too much magnificence in which I long be a part of. If the day comes of my prospering in moderate riches, I will appreciate every cent while holding on to the past as a reminder of my once-upon-a-time monetary hardships. Money will not darken my soul, and from that alone I truly believe I can succeed.

Finally, I would like the opportunity to release from my thoughts one last image that has been smothered by the clutches of my subconscious mind. I have forever aspired to hold a piece of the honor that comes with helping to preserve this illustrious world we inhabit. I truly believe that my purpose is to ultimately achieve this illusion that fantasies itself in my mind, but the fight to survive alone is a challenge that is presented as an overwhelming obstacle only to be achieved by those who can strengthen their being with raw courage. Shall I remove my blinders that fancy a pleasantville world, I will face the reality that each passing day accompanies a disintegration of our longing to embrace each other with our hands filled with peace.

Keeping this in mind, I must choose my battles carefully, for not everything can be fixed by my own desire to heroically barricade the gifted from chaos. I am a lost soul who bears a great deal of remorse for a losing battle that is far beyond my control. I want to protect the innocent while combating the demons, but my focus is on saving those who remain silenced by a lack of sheer importance. Somehow I will make a difference on this planet, while resisting ridicule by those who lack the power of acceptance. I will not allow anyone to strip me of my willpower, my strength, and my determination to succeed in a day where expectations have become defined by a stereotype versus a necessity to survive.

I can only hope to achieve greatness in all of the areas of my life deemed important under the guidelines of my own expectations. However, if one of my many prospects lingers to the side of failure, I must find the poetry within the depths of my being to be thankful for the gifts I have received instead of withering in self pity over what was not destined to be. As long as I have faith in my own abilities, I will accomplish any goal set forth on my journey through this adventurous opportunity known as life. I will not cower in shame over my current state of existence, often compared to a highly overrated universal stature set by others. When I do reach the peak of my venture, I will hold my head high, for I can be sure that my path was quilted and composed from the standards that were created out of my own desire to attain my personal best. I will forever remember what is important in life, because I will not settle for any less commitment from my inner self worth. I will not allow my insecurities to become a blazing inferno that destroys this once in a lifetime possibility in the here and now. I am a survivor, I am a believer, I will be my biggest supporter through my own eyes, and I will do this all for a dreamer who is better known to me as; my self.

CHAPTER 19

NOT FIT TO OWN A COW PATTY

The dilemma during this chapter is one that is to be ignored by a voluntarily blind and callous society. An entire epidemic of impetuous pet owners are permitted, by all acts of free will, to snatch an animal of various sorts and enforce upon it any behavior they deem as an appropriate act of good conscience. To no great surprise, many of these pseudo caretakers lack the personal intellect it requires to satisfy their own daily survival needs, more or less the common sense involved in caring for a creature that just so happened to be in the wrong place at a very inopportune moment. The only time intervention is executed by an outside force is when the feces is knee deep, or a frozen critter at the end of its chain is coincidentally spotted by a passerby. Apparently this mournful display of negligence wasn't noticed anytime prior, or as reality would prove, a great deal of human tail tucking was easier than picking up that inventive little communication unit that allows us to transmit our voice from one location to the next. Therefore, I have made the decision to verbally paint my words of utter disgust across the next few pages. My intention is to slap a little reality across the faces of those who have the audacity to declare themselves worthy enough to care for our innocent, fair-haired, delicate souls of the domesticated animal kingdom. In order for me to accurately prove my point, I am going to narrate for you a rather in-depth scenario.

A finger-to-toe stretch and a mouthful of stale air is all the inspiration you need for a bright idea; as you finally awaken from the comfort of you sleep zone during this mid afternoon. The brain is frantically at work, and what a miraculous turn of events this is considering the cobwebs have grown significantly thick within the parameters of your numb skull. When you're greeted by your maniac children at the bedroom door, you can barely contain your own excitement as the words "let's get a dog", frantically spew from the edge of your tongue. The atmosphere instantly fills with the sound of high pitched screams as the children start drop kicking each other in a race that is rewarded by the honorary front seat of the car privilege. As you come rolling up to the animal prison, where the most unwanted are routinely executed, your brilliant strategy of keeping the rugrats out of your hair, is suddenly clouded with a cumbering emotion of regret. This negative mood soon fades as you proudly stand aside and watch your children sprint up and down the jail cell aisles like you've just doped each of them with two gallons of high speed caffeine. After an hour has vanished you have at last pronounced which of the over excited canines, who are all currently in a provoked state of runaway urination liberation, has won today's human lottery jackpot. Today's lucky winner is a Heinz 57 inbred, sporting multicolored eyes, and a fur coat that is full of matted dreadlocks. Instantly the name Jack Daniel's flashes through your mind like a bad acid trip, so you bellow his entitlement from the top of your lungs in a state of overwhelming self gratification. Your psychotic little people each have their own designated pooch call, so you've reached the conclusion that the dog has a premiere name with a whole slew of ingenious nicknames. This remarkable turn of events will only prove to the rest of the population that stupidity is the dominant gene running through your family. Finally you've arrived back at the home front, and sparing little time, you immediately introduce the new relative to his new headquarters. This manmade luxury was previously derived out of plywood, and it remains full of warmed-over bedding from last year's bright idea. You clasp his 10ft. freedom chain around his neck and barely acknowledge his presence from that day forward; except of course to holler a few words of silence during his nonstop barking crusades. Your mangy children have developed a feeling of despise for the mutt, because the daily feedings are interrupting their via live wrestling matches that take place in the living room on a regular basis. The dog is now loathed, the kids have evolved into full blown boredom by his mere presence, and you are a bitter and cynical pet owner who should have followed your first instinct of retreat now before it's too late.

Now let us embrace this moment and seize the opportunity to direct your attention towards the persecution single handily executed upon this delinquent animal friend. Every morning Jack is abruptly aroused from a brutal night's sleep by the clamor of two kettle pots being recklessly hurled to the ground. As his cruel half-wit owner hastily paces back to his useless existence that spares little room for quality brain function, Jack scurries to the water hole that is quickly evaporating into the ground. After a few muddy laps with his tongue, the hound stretches across to the second spilled over pot and chomps down a few rock hard morsels that are better known to him as breakfast, lunch, and dinner. His days are consumed by utter loneliness which provokes him to fill the air with the sound of his broken hearted melody of endless barking. The sultry days of summer are merciless as his thick fur coat absorbs every bit of the blistering heat. The morning water hole spares just enough liquid replenishment to prevent complete dehydration from securing Jack's threshold on death. Although this unyielding solstice seems like the inevitable role call for departing souls, this unforgiving season pales in comparison to the bitter display presented by the winter months. Water is plentiful during these everlasting weeks as helpless Jack rapidly licks the formation of ice from the end of his frost coated paws. As each frigid night approaches, the feel of hypothermia lingers in the background, and the pup wraps in a fetal positions to protect himself against the arctic air. He whimpers with despair in his tone, and the sound of his own cry is the only realization that life is but another breath away. In his sleep Jack dreams of a place where he is honored with a full meal and a cozy place to sleep. Little did he realize, what came to him in his nighttime illusion was the prison from which he was first brought home. A duration where his fate was doomed by execution becomes a fantasy in comparison to his current state of existence.

These types of repulsive actions displayed by the human culture are truly a collection of genuine tragedies, and this type of negligence is openly accepted by our willingness to ignore what can be changed with little effort. What an outrage it is to know that any person in our society has the right to become a pet owner, regardless of their reckless and negligent history as a careless provider. For those of you who fit the character described in my previous scenario, you do not deserve the privilege of having animal custody. However, you have earned the right to sleep in a cardboard box during the middle of a brisk winter, and you have also earned the right to serve a similar sentence like the one you have imposed on an innocent creature. Lacking common sense is simply a refusal to acknowledge your commitment. Utilizing this trait automatically informs you that if you are at your wits end with the animal, then have enough audacity to find him a proper home. Tying him outside while waiting for the inevitable to occur is simply an act exercised by an anal retentive moron who has developed very little respect for life in general. I am baffled by this universal ignorance, and I am even more ashamed to be a part of a society that voluntarily turns a blind eye. Here ye here ye, is there a member of our society who could enlighten me on the phonics of pet care responsibility, and then fully explain how one evolves into a belligerent menace while providing for the beautiful innocence that depends solely on our ability to nurture? Here is a baffling concept for you to inherit as a part of your birth to intelligence. Animals cannot perform culinary art inside you kitchen, nor will they initiate proper household companionship by inserting a how to video inside the VCR. Let's compare this little adventure to raising the children. When your neonate is born, you don't just bring him home, plop him in the baby carriage, and then wait for an invitation to his graduation. Obviously there is an enormous amount of love, caring, patience, teaching, and providing, while traveling down the road that leads to this magnificent celebration of independence. Using these same fundamentals, while raising your critter, should rate as an equal priority in order for everyone involved to splendor in a fruitful existence. There is a wide variety of elegant and precious critters waiting to be adopted by a caring family. However, in the wrong hands, any creature can be molded into an endangered species that most would sacrifice to euthanasia, rather than intervene with the intent to protect. What a sorrowing attitude we have chosen to embrace, and a horrifying concept that continues to thrive.

CHAPTER 20

WAR OF THE PRIMITIVELY ANTISOCIAL

During this particular chapter I have chosen to depict three of the most infamous controversies from our unforgiving and emotionally impotent society. Thus, I shall open a can of worms for all members of human diversity to feed on. Then I will enforce an open-eyed look at a neglected dilemma; the truth of which is being suffocated by a whole rash of blameworthy citizens who freely hand out a pamphlet of infantile excuses to ease their guilty conscience. I will linger on each topic long enough to obtain my very own hate mail post office box, but you should keep in mind that I don't have one, so you may want to exercise this wasted energy of boiling hatred elsewhere. The first subject I will attack, with the intention of stimulating premature hair growth, is the ingenious view of racial armageddon suggested by the paranoid instincts of the skin head nazis. Then I will stroll through the pastures of the mad cow extremists who would rather share in the thrill of farm animal penetration versus fondling a member of their own genital liking. Finally, after I give an indiscreet bow to the absent-minded intellect of a time warped male, I will conclude this chapter of human disgrace with a bit of attention in honor of the handicapped persons who inspire this world. I shall not deliver a promise which would entail my sentences to be fancied with kind words, and I would not have to burn these bridges if the issues were not a fuel that is igniting a pit of blazing hatred in the realm of the human soul. I have chosen to rise above the use of violence to express my viewpoints, and I will leave this form of rage to the cowards who spare little room for intellectual retaliation.

The human complexion is a veil which shrouds the deep-rooted abomination brought forth by the dictatorship of the skin head nazis. A society which feeds off of the misguided direction of their masters is defiant to the reality of this world, and ultimately they have been brainwashed by the mentally insane. Allow me to clue you in on common knowledge that is uprooting the foundation of your contention. You are a self promoting universal cult that insists on the conjoining of white power. However, your intentions are in a full force backlash that is forming an alliance between all races who do not grasp the concept behind your backwoods plan to mass procreate an inbred lineage. Your attempt to empower the white race is suffering because you are the center of your own humiliation. Repetitive words of racial fury continue to spew from the gaping hole in the center of you skulls, while the general population sits in awe as if they were observing an extraterrestrial mammal on display in a third world country petting zoo. Not to mention what a horrific disgrace it is to know that you're on an endless spawning crusade to instill your anti morals in the minds of innocent children. This unorthodox fraternity envelopes its ego with the sound of self applause, and at the same time, they are wasting valuable oxygen by turning it into verbal pollution. The baffling part of this dilemma is that a whole cluster of followers have united to promote a cause that lapsed into an eternal coma along with Hitler, yet they continue to thrive by initiating weak minded failures who are easily influenced by anyone who glosses them with attention. Before I gracefully exit this paragraph I must declare, for the sake of the sane, that a majority of us were bred from the moderately intellectual white class, and we prefer to form an opinion based on our own ability to interpret the rest of society. Therefore, we would appreciate universal silence from a group of citizens who do not represent the majority. If you are that desperate to belong, then do the world a favor by gathering in a room on a certain date, shave your heads completely bald, wear the exact same outfits, and drink a large glass of tainted Kool-Aid. I am convinced it worked for the previous anti-intellectual cults.

Next I shall draw attention to a well known universal secret that is intentionally concealed so that the world continues to ride this abnormal merry-go-round; better known as life. This cloak-

and-dagger mystery that is ignored by virtually all human species, divulges that men and women will never find the hidden fortune of empathy by reading each other's treasure map. We simply coexist because somewhere along the ancestry timeline an idea was initiated, which included two of the most diverse genders on this planet. These opposite genders were to find a way to continually replenish this world with the likes of each other. However, during the course of time a few of the signals became crossed, and this formed the creation of same sex partners who fully understood the physical and mental structure of their newfound mate. You see, I believe what lesbians have found in one another, is a similar human creation bound by patience, honesty, sincerity, emotional well-being, empathy, and nurturing; which are foreign traits to the male population. The homosexual culture is the link to interdependent bliss because each partner was originally cut from the same mold. This type of virtual equality radiates in comparison to sorting through the mayhem created when very opposite genders spend their entire lives trying to master two separate puzzles with intention of creating one giant picture. I am a heterosexual female who is forced to spend a lifetime trying to decode the hand guide to male intelligence; which by the way was constructed and printed using some sort of foreign masculine dialect. Therefore, I can only imagine how phenomenally compatible a same sex partnership must be, and unfortunately I will never experience this sort of ecstasy because my signals never rewired into normalcy. I am unable to speak for homosexual males only because I have never unlocked the mystery behind the entire gender, yet I am still convinced that gay men must share in some sort of biological understanding just the same as females do. Being that I am a creature of this planet, I haven't any doubt that an inferno-sized flame has been sparked in the derriere of the anti-crusade population, and since we already know how uptight they feel about their anus, I am sure the enema business will soon fall into bankruptcy. At any rate, I shall leave you with a bit of tainted knowledge that you can belly up on during your next adventure to straight man's land. Explore the alienation of a new anti hobby, because the homosexuals will far outlive heterosexuals due to their experience with a unique human connection that we shall never embrace.

The next subject I am campaigning for, as an attribute to the entire female liberation cause, will wholeheartedly focus on the heroic triumph inspired from an enormous amount of raw courage and estrogen-based strength. We as the female population have risen above all human expectations to enhance a rank in society that was forbidden in an era of forgotten time. It seems that nobody dares to examine the one form of servitude that is rarely acknowledged in today's day and age, because this form of betrayal would divulge an epoch of time when a woman ministered to the beck and call of her master. That particular chronicle of our past has simply been discounted as a way of life because of the harsh realities suffered during the time of the African American slavery's. Let the fact remain that our ancestors were degraded like worthless species who endured a life that spared very little promise for any personal aspirations and goals. However, we as females have fully recognized that rigorous past, and we have striven to eclipse all of our obstacles, which ultimately led us to a prosperous life fulfilled by our own willingness to achieve beyond all expectations. We refuse to become strangled by a past that seemed hopeless, and we choose to engender any obstacle as a stepping stone towards our future. Although our world still inhabits a small percentage of old school men, our deeply rooted potency has united us on a common ground which cannot be destroyed by any man's callous ideals. We are the women of this world, thus we will fight to conquer the spineless who thrive on degrading our persistence, and this alone is the driving power towards fully empowering our own gender.

Last but not least, I will address one final issue that is deemed unimportant to all of the inhabitants who convey limited regard for the motivation, determination, and mutual respect which this country was founded on. I would like to honor this world with special regards to all of the disabled who have risen above their handicaps, thus they have blessed us with the power of inspiration beyond what any other human can provide. These folks are the true survivors of trial over tribulation, and they are a heroic role model for any mortal to admire. However, as they have chosen not to accept society's pity and charitable handouts, I feel the need to draw attention towards a predicament that has cause for verbal retaliation. If you are a perfectly capable and fully active human being, than have enough decency and self pride to find a parking spot that is not specifically marked handicapped. Now I realize this means you may have to remove yourself from being perpetually indolent. However, if you take advantage of this moment, you will be able to subscribe to a bit of brain utilization which will provide to you an interaction with the function of judgement that issues the determining factor between right and wrong. In any case, I fully intend to interpret the specifics behind this world wide plan to end an informal abuse that most cretins have become knowingly oblivious to. This means that you cannot park in a handicap location for the purpose of briefly running into the store to pick up a few odds and ends, or to drop off a video. Maneuvering your automobile half cocked in their parking spaces also qualifies you as a guilty party along with the rest of the half-wit population; whose ultimate goal outwits their logical thinking. I am fully aware that a majority of our society has succumbed to a laziness which will delay our goal to achieve excellence in the common sense department while embarking on the new millennium. Therefore I can only hope, by repetitiously dwelling on this dilemma, that eventually the fright of equal ignorance will erode your hardened conscience the next time your thought process becomes abducted by lethargy. If you feel panicked by your body's reaction to exercise, then perhaps one's self would be more comfortable living a paraplegic, and maybe you could consult them on how rewarding close parking is in comparison to an extensive walk.

Ladies and gentlemen, in spite of my overdose of sarcasm, it seems so painfully clear that spreading around mutual respect would be a healthier and more productive living arrangement versus a life that is seething on hostility. Unfortunately the messengers of twisted mentality are in a race to thrash their enemy, so our future sanity will have to depend on the intervention of a stable mind. What a shame it is to know that we are a society who chooses an existence disjoined by each individual's distinct human qualities, rather than enhancing humanity with an overall acceptance derived from this miraculous gift of life. We are all unique sovereignties in our own right who share in common the reality of being within the same species, and regardless of your racist opinion, it is a matter of fact that will remain eternal despite your insistence to separate. HATE! HATE! HATE! HATE! HATE! Is this really how we want to live?

CHAPTER 21

A GIFT FROM MOTHER EARTH

I would like to dedicate this chapter to the essence of life and the miraculous wonders of fate. I have chosen to invalidate all of the self righteous mayhem hand delivered by human carelessness, and I shall highlight the next few pages with a picturesque view in celebration of this ravishing habitat we call earth. Digging through the endless tribulations of human chaos can be presented without challenge, but to remove one's ego from the big picture and envision life through the eyes of mother nature, is a fresh and stimulating invitation in itself. We can always define one another and the place we inhabit by a description of a callused blemish, but having the mind power to seek beyond the superficial is what I have chosen to elaborate on. My purpose is to present an enlightened vision of a world that is so often taken for granted, and depict a life that is coupled by variety and magnificence that most have chosen to see blinded. Accept my words for the beauty they represent, or remain hardened by my previously insensitive representation of the human race, but embrace the opportunity to understand, respect, and relish a world that we have so easily forgotten to love. Take a tour on this journey through the four seasons, and we shall bond with our inhabitance through an enlightened perspective. At the close of our pages may we reach a common ground cradled by a universal admiration.

A pleasant sprinkle of morning dew glosses the birth of our flourishing cosmic garden. Shower filled clouds are gracefully poised within the midst of the everlasting skyline, and the birds of melody harmonically carol a wildlife song to theatrically present the approaching frolic of springtime raindrops. The blossoming of all natural, bouquets the earth as the persistence of a winter finale fades in the night. The balance of a mystical earth that accompanies each spring day and eve brings with it a sense of enchantment that no other season can parallel. The hibernation of life during a shivery and elongated winter is aroused by an invisible caress of seasonal warmth. All variation of colors begin to flare, while each distinctive hue becomes flattered by the next. Without any permission a tap dancing rain show drums a performance on all that is exposed, thus each of mother earth's decorations become blessed by a refreshing drink from the fountain in the sky. The sun frolics in a game of hide and seek, as each separated cloud allows for a quick glimpse of the prospering environment below. We shall shun the rain as it pours to the ground, and we shall praise the fire in the sky as it attempts to shine through, but always remember that each miraculous event works hand in hand to create this magnificent, earth filled garden.

As one season bows to the arrival of the next, a sensation of intensity penetrates the atmosphere. The blazing inferno in the sky wraps its arms around the earth below, and the prolonged daylight is filled by the relentless and sultry summer heat. The essence of life absorbs the fevered rays while the trickle of perspiration alleviates the sweltering of all that desire relief. The cloud-vacant sky soon embraces darkness, for as quickly as the sun stimulated daylight, the deceptive masquerade casts a darkened image on the earth below. During a bout with utter magnificence this cluster of onyx evolves into a miraculous downward spiral brought forth by the potency of Mother Nature. She roars like a reckless freight train, thus striking out with relentless arms of electricity that assault all who cast a dare. Her fury within will shame all technology, and her moment of conclusion will only be determined when a victory is secured by the act of submission. She vanishes in the moment, thus leaving her imprint on a path defined by retribution. The tempest settles, dissipating within the realm of her element, and a vast array of calm quickly attends to all that is frightened. The sensuous summer will affix upon us a cradling comfort and a serenity that offers an occasion brought forth by the boundary of respect. The essence of life is captured by the glistening of the stars, and the earth is highlighted by the brightened moonlight radiating in the nighttime sky. Although she forecasts peril with a vengeance, she is the only season to bestow excellence after a moment of fear.

As the days quickly journey to a place enhanced by the next phase, another summery season bleeds into the fragrance of fall. The atmosphere submits to a cooling breeze allowing for a temperate comfort to nestle all creatures who encountered the sweltering heat lamp from above. The critters of the wild relentlessly forage in preparation for the everlasting slumber months to follow, and the picturesque leaves colorfully wave farewell as they're whisked away by the autumn zephyr. The falling rain catches a chill, and all who bear habitation begin to synthesize as an attempt to forethink the fade of revitalization until the dawn of the new arrives once again. The crests of the water swish to the shoreline bringing with it a chill, thus forewarning the waterfowl that the months to follow will frame it in the shape of a frigid glass mirror. Fly away to the land where the aquatics are tepid, and fortune the sapphire sky that welcomes you in a cradle of warmth. The atmosphere appears to be dramatizing a forever perish, but Mother Nature is simply nurturing the environment in preparation for what is to follow. We have been honored by a season that tenders to peace in the here and now, yet in a naturalistic sequence, she portrays a suggestion of the imminent.

All remains serene in the land of the frigid after a tyrannizing blizzard stakes claim on the unexpected. The tree branches appear lethargic yet concentrated while burdening the import of a relentless wintry snowfall. The air lingers in the atmosphere with an arctic impression, and the breath of the living is a visual representation that all creation will continue to flourish. The lakes are in a state of polarized tranquility, and the cold-blooded creatures of the underworld exist in an ordinary seclusion that is far removed from the rest of the living. The landscape is garnished with a stunning array of frosted icicles, and the soil becomes the foundation for a variety of glacial-coated pyramids. You can retire from the cold or defy it, but the ultimate dare is to create an everlasting heat source that will offer security to one's survival in this brisk winter wonderland. The dauntless inferno appears to have warranted its distance, thus yielding to the animation of old man winter. He grasps his adventure by fanning out in a blanket of unremitting, billowy fluff, and the world soon becomes a cattle of servants that enact submission in his almighty presence. Innocence is his act of disguise, but vigor is his true color that prospers over this sugarcoated visage.

It is rather unfortunate that we as the human race have become so cross-grained during the tour of our seasons, particularly when they flaunt their miraculous potential. Each of the four seasons has a spectacular exhibition for us to embrace as a phenomenal and scenic expression of life. Unfortunately, the world chooses to spawn a negative critique that depicts altogether the seasons' distinct qualities, and we categorize them into a state of wretched downfalls. Imagine if the world had been painted using only black and white, thus leaving aside the physical feeling and eye-capturing beauty that is emitted by the ambiance of each wondrous season. Appreciate the habitat that is presented before you, because life is far too brief in time to envision it any other way.

CHAPTER 22

SUE THIS!

In my previous chapter I became drawn into a tip toeing happy dance through the lily fields, when suddenly the depths of reality came crashing in on my pretty party. Instantly I became aware of my fundamental purpose which involves a radical goal that details the harsh realities of our present existence, and I realized that I must continue to focus on humanities self destruction. Therefore, I would like to welcome you all to the day and age where we have become so preoccupied by greed, that our actions have literally superceded our intellectual rank. In any case, I have come to the conclusion that the farther we strive to achieve greatness; ultimately, we are retrogressing by outwitting this predetermined desire. During this particular segment I am recalling our lost mentality in hopes of regaining a sense of universal pride. Since we as a society have become virtually engrossed in the idea of irrational courtroom drama, I will spend the next few pages dwelling on the fraternity of mindless lawsuits. I will also discuss how the demise of our superiority spawned from all of the radical court awarded decisions. Before I begin my journey of demented word spewing, I must first dispense a piece of acknowledgement towards the lawsuits that expel the underlying purpose of the jurisdictions, and mediate using rightful interjection between these deceitful mishaps. A great deal of historical prosecution was exercised with the idea of mindful resolution and honest intent, however, the nineties version of a courtroom melodrama can better be described as a barnyard soap opera that is openly displayed for public viewing and superficial ratings. The happily-ever-after tale usually concludes, following an over-dramatized tattle fest, when one party consummates the hearing by walking away with a self promoting reward that stemmed from disgorging their opponent's indecent personal life. On the other hand, the world is being stalked by such a wide variety of crooked thieves, that the words deceit and fraud have literally become the central support system for the mockery and demoralization of our once respected courtrooms. Besides human mockery, we have also completely undermined our overall intelligence by forcing most business enterprises into securing a common sense warning to any product that makes an appearance on the department store shelves. These boldly printed labels have become so degrading that a well detailed picture diagram is affixed, proposing to the consumer, the proper way to utilize a product without causing themselves great bodily harm. Last but not least, while we're dwelling on the tragic loss of rationale within the judicial and human network, I would like to point out a travesty that has developed from all of this chaotic mayhem. If a fellow patron encounters a life threatening incident that requires immediate medical attention, I am afraid the person might die because no one would dare to volunteer their assistance. You see, we as a society have literally become callused by fear. If helping someone out means that we may encounter a multi-million dollar suit that eliminates our financial well being, then a blind eye is simply an easier way to remain bankrupt free. Unfortunately this only proves to illustrate the bottomless pit we are wallowing around in, and needless to say, I have discovered yet another idiocy to inherently dissect.

First of all I must begin my weak-minded human crusade by exposing all of these fatuous lawsuits that are hemorrhaging into the courtrooms at a colossal rate. We as a society like to cry victim every time our space is invaded with the stench of a fellow patron, and not only have we glorified this social disgrace, but now we can witness this waste of air time on every major network television station. These corporate geniuses have basically discovered a lucrative way to capitalize on our human idiocies. That fact alone strikes a nerve in my curiously deceptive brain, simply because nearly every person who enters a televised court facility just so happens to be an impeccable half-wit whose primary goal involves fifteen minute fame-sucking. It is very hard to determine which of these two factors is more ingenious, rather, is it that the plaintiff and defendant are battling over lawn trash space, or is it that both of these nitwits voluntarily stand in front of the human version of stain who relentlessly batters them into submissions? Unlike the multimillion dollar cases fraudulently claimed every couple of weeks, these folks should not be entering our courtrooms with the intention of finding a life's career calling. Therefore, instead of existing in a world that cannot afford your presence, simply extinguish the brush fire, and return to your homes.

On that note, allow me to indulge your mind in a brief paragraph that explains to the world why consumer enterprises are forced to belittle our intelligence every time a new product is introduced, or an old product is revised for the sake of our personal safety. Let me envision for you a quick and simple example of how this remarkable turn of events tends to evolve. When you order a cup of coffee from a quickie drive-thru, I would encourage society to read and understand the warning label that signifies hot contents. Unfortunately, due to a hot crotch lawsuit that erupted some time ago, this common sense label is marked on the side of every styrofoam cup. I would like to accredit a majority of society for upholding the knowledge that openly indicates the avoidance of using your thighs as a cup holder for any scalding hot liquid. However, if you're unclear about this common sense knowledge, then I would highly recommend bathing in hot coffee, followed by a brief visit to the nearest hospital for a band aid, and then stop by the courts for your lotto-sized restitution. Now, most fellow readers are probably insulted at this point by my representation of an accident that turned the world into a destructive blaze of weak-minded infantiles. However, you must also keep in mind, if product distributors did not take the time to print these labels, some freak of nature would be ignorant enough bathe with his electronic CD player.

On the other hand, the burnt thighs cretins of the world hardly lift a finger to bask in millions, simply because there are leeches (better known as lawyers) waiting in the cracks for these pitiful, body blistered, backwoods junkies to slink into their offices. These money hungry society slugs see an opportunity to advance financially from one tax bracket to the next. Following their daydreaming encounter with notoriety, these lawyers prepare heartfelt and over dramatized presentations that are backed by inventive statistics. The jury is brainwashed by three day histrionics that are filled with a disturbing array of lifelong travesties the plaintiffs have endured, which ultimately led them down a path of reckless decision making. Thus, when the smoke clears and the theatrics subside, the pitiful clients walk away with millions of dollars. To sum up a relentless paragraph which explicitly details why corporate America treats society like half-wit inbreeds, well just ask Nancy Numbskull who walked away with their annual bottom line. Remember boys and girls, don't blow dry your hair in the shower, always remove the plastic from your food before cooking, and never ever light a cigarette while spraying your bouffant.

I hardly want to display the impression that our entire court system is completely incoherent, or that we as the habitually existent should not fight for what is rightfully ours. Unfortunately we are basking in an epoch of time where people have embraced the idea of dishonesty rather than virtue. The courts are merely acting as the parent to an entire society of grown children with tainted values, and the system is being grossly taken advantage of. Besides, without the intervention of the court system, we would literally undergo free for all duping from a society that has inherited the concept of *though shall financially rape thy neighbor.*

The problem stems from an entire cluster of anti-educated liberals who are under the impression that they have been burdened by a form of superior intellect to which the rest of the world is foreign. Therefore, they exist by betraying the common folk, who in reality, could sport a brain the size of a peanut, and still bear a higher degree of common knowledge. This is proven to be true simply by the amount of court hearings that are generated by the average Joe, and these lawsuits are usually against a self proclaimed genius who swindled his way right into the courtroom. Although a handful of these career seeking, lackluster, cheats, may slither away with societies greenbacks, I wouldn't suggest depositing the idea into your numbskull. Remember, in the end, the only reward you will reap is that of consequence. Eventually the government will cease the act of frivolous hoodwinking, and an entire rash of opportunists will have to crawl back into the woodwork. Not to mention the fact that the government will have to step further into our personal lives and make lawful decisions that we have become too engrossed to enact. The web for deceit has been set in motion, and the skin that crawls is the key for entrapment.

There is one last quagmire I must dwell on before the closing of this chapter. Thanks to this vast eruption of inferior battling inside every civil courtroom, the priority of attending to our immediate health has become significantly marred in the eyes of the ordinary being. Allow me the pleasure of introducing to you a brief scenario that spawned from our day and age. During a crowded dining out, a fellow patron has slipped onto the ground enduring a backbone breakage and a severe head injury. Although the man has blood seeping from every orifice, the spectators have chosen to call an ambulance, and observe from a safe distance. The reason society has become skeptical about offering immediate assistance, is because they fear they could be sued by the family if the man dies while in their care. I am hardly proclaiming that this is a reaction that occurs during every medical emergency, but a fear in the public's mind has been created, and a person's life could become at an even greater risk due to this societal panic. Unfortunately this kind of terror attack is lurking in the realm of our domain, because the case in point has been justified by the court system during the very first multimillion dollar award. If the court is proposing to the world a lesson to be taught through the use of money, I hardly think financial rape is the way to punish authentic intentions. The fact of the matter remains that if you are permitting one family to retire from another man's honest means of conduct, then basically you are giving permission to the rest of society to act on this disrepute.

My entire point for this segment was to deliver a few eye-opening pages with the intention of choke holding our tainted ideals of right and wrong. Instead of enduring a time of caution towards our neighbors and peers, we should embrace the concept of an open arm relationship through the power offered by our hearts and our minds. A time of need will approach every being, and should we encounter such a problem, one's ego shall stand alone because of a previous encounter with dishonest intent, or you will be conjoined in a blessed event that evolved from a life represented by self contribution. If the court systems continue to award retirement to any cluster schmuck who stalks this planet, then we may as well bow to the likes of ignorance as our new means of social rectitude. Our conscience as a whole has frozen into a stone cold community which is setting into a wretched molding, not only for our future, but as a chapter in our history. Basically, we are choosing to neglect our intelligence potency by openly displaying an entire wash of ignorant conduct. We may very well be the superior intellectual species, if that constitutes outwitting our ability to enact productive thinking and applying it to effectual behavior. Unless we are willing to enact the concept of self analysis and personal growth, we will unquestionably go down in history as the society who became the most mentally cannibalistic of our day.

CHAPTER 23

GENERATION IMMORTALITY

Our society has conquered the unthinkable, but achieving these great lengths has created a horrendous path of destruction with nothing left unscathed. Nothing on earth is secured by a sense of serene protection as long as our immortality remains in question, and in a matter of our surreal fated destiny, the answer shall be drawn from the depths of denial in an unspoken reality.

During this awakening of moral servitude I shall verbalize a cause that is destined to strike fury in the minds of the weak, and I shall single out those who are impotent towards the enlightenment of all natural diversity. The blinders we wear have blackened a miraculous opportunity to truly see life at its finest, and we are shaded in our effort to find experience in a place that is beyond fascination. Therefore, I have chosen to speak of a forbidden subject and I shall do so without delivering a shield of caution. My hope is that in the end I will have sparked the flame that lights upon variation. I will address the underlying controversy that has shadowed the fight to remain forever existent, and I shall interpret my own cause worthy beliefs that remain unfounded to a callous world. Although I shall infuriate a collection of anti animal stalkers, I have chosen to front forward my helpless crusade without fearing the inevitable enemies; thus they will ultimately outnumber my compassionate allies. My ensuing issue with our society is founded from the idea that we will gallantly strive to defeat the question of mortality by destroying and experimenting on all of the human-pronounced lesser species. I am sitting on a series of dead end crossroads with the issue of sustaining our human rights as uncivil beings. Thus, we are ultimately permitting ourselves to maliciously destroy the earth and the species within. This form of hypocritical hierarchy is simply an attempt to preserve the longevity of human life - regardless of the sacrifice involved. I truly cherish god, and although he has supplied our need to survive with various provisions, I strongly disbelieve that this offering was given to us as an opportunity to exist forever. We have sorely taken advantage of our gifts, and in the end our selfish acts will reap the consequence from our creator. Shall we embrace a life of greed developed from self-induced disease, surely the day will embark upon us a form of retribution beyond technological domination.

Secondly, I am determined through open protest to shed a blinding light on our aching desire to become superficially beautiful through the eyes of our own skin-deep scrutiny. This form of universal cult conformity has become a matter of social acceptance through a horrific sacrifice of the innocent. We have not been granted superiority for the purpose of abusing this unbounded power, and our desperate attempt to glorify perfection and defy mortality at any expense will eventually suffer at the hands unequaled retaliation.

Although miraculous discoveries have transpired through the mysteries of science, this extraordinary feat to grasp immortality has been accomplished at the expense of all wondrous creatures and the exotics of this land. It seems that we have disadvantaged our ability to find cures for the impossible by ensuing a scenic-routed entanglement, thus we are blindly being led back to the place where first began. I wouldn't eat an apple in order to unveil the essence of an orange, and as theoretically simple as that may be, this same retrogressive misjudgment is being propagated by the scientific community every single day. I dare not challenge the phenomenon that has come thus far through animal experimentation, but the amount of time being squandered, when the same results could have been proven earlier through a more sensible and reliable means, is the true controversy at hand. Ladies and gentlemen, I urge you to take a long, hard look in the mirror, and I will assure you that an image of whiskers and a fur coated body will not be the reflected vision ogling back at you. The reason the FDA approved product is pulled off of the market, rendered hazardous to your health, is because the cure in question is not being tested on the species intended for its use. If we are so desperately eager to find a miracle antidote to remedy our own self-inflicted diseases, then we should be equally impassioned to volunteer our own superficial beings instead of maiming the rest of the innocent and uninvolved species. Our hypocritical disposition on life promotes victimizing the natural world. Instead, we should be focusing our attention on the prisons that are full of ruthless criminals who could be giving back to society through a punishment of scientific experimentation sentencing. We have institutionalized the Frankenstein style of medical science on an entirely incorrect collection of species. If you want to test a worthy and reliable theory on a casualty of science then employ your resources on the slugs of our society, thus you must release the innocent from your twisted clutches. Growing a human body part on the back of a rodent is a horrific display of ignorance, especially when you could apply this trial and error technique on an actual human being who is rotting behind the walls of a maximum security prison. Allow me to enlighten you with my own warped theory in regards to the criminally insane, tax sponging junkies of our time. Take the entire cluster of child molesting perverts and grow a genital on their backsides. Then, during prison recess you can toss this scientifically developed pansy out into the prison playground. Thus, this remarkable feat would allow for him to be fondled against his will by a group of desperate, male seeking, horny-toads. The millions of tax dollars relinquished yearly could be combined from both science and federal prisons to form an eternal budget that leads to quick and accurate results. The illegitimate members of our society could finally be sentenced to a punishment that actually fits their crime. Have we become so self-righteous, even during a chance encounter with death and disease, that we will forever refuse to sacrifice the human body in order to recover? If our ultimate goal is exist parallel to eternity then self sacrifice is the inevitable answer without question.

Once upon a time in a thought process exceeding our present day spell, beauty was looked at beyond vanity, and it was dignified with a stroke of admiration. Ironically enough, beauty eventually became the root of our insecure evils. Glamour has been proven to arise from sacrifice, however, the victim of virtue is ruled by the hand of perfection. We have become the true cowards in the battle against superficiality, and our legacy will be written in stone depicting our ability and desire to destroy all means of life for our personal gain. Poison, mutilation, and death are inflicted on all species beneath the human domain, and with self granted permission, the creatures of the here and now will become tomorrow's prey and sacrifice; all in the name of beauty. When the human race empowers themselves to dictate beauty; fear and mistrust will be implanted in the minds of the weak. They are the species of misfortune placed in a world without care, and their place in the animal kingdom has become a stomping ground for human needs. If worshiping vanity is the goal of our time then stand in line for self ruin, but terminate the destruction of animals and their domain. Beauty is not the definition of survival, and persecution of the weaker species through human-induced experimentation is not the power we were given permission to maliciously abuse.

We as the consumer are the benefactors in this humiliating attempt to prolong our youth, and with our generous greenbacks the demon-ruled industries will continue to wreak havoc on the misfortunes of coincidence. The commercialized corporations of perfected beauty products have become the subliminal masters of foolery, and we as the naïve consumers have peddled away our dignity by selling out the natural world for the price of supposed elegance. These monstrous corporations would be basking in the pity of bankruptcy if the consumer wasn't being blindsided by the glamour commercials. We are endlessly force-fed the misleading and superficial morals of the entire beauty industry. I strongly believe that a very minute percentage of our population would continue to indulge in beauty products if the revelation of truth in animal experimentation was required in the currently deceptive television advertisements. However, our day and age of self-serving imbeciles has become so gratifying, that a message of any gross intensity may not be enough to tempt the cold barriers blocking our path to compassionate living. As the chambers of horrific terror and torture have become unthinkable in light of humanitarianism, this same form of benevolence should be upheld towards all species. Acknowledgement is the first step in recovery, and denial is the last step in shame.

To conclude yet another chronicle in the pages of history, I would like to leave you with this. The world that cradles the environment within is but a fated bout with miraculous wonderment, yet we are callous to the teardrops and to the shrill call of all who will remain silent among deaf ears. I refuse to negate that each person as an individual exists not wanting a destination that evolves into an eternal life, but this passion with hope must be obtained by our own willingness to self sacrifice, rather than voluntarily victimizing those without a voice to be heard at all. To ultimately achieve immortal victory by using the defenseless as our stepping stone is a battle which holds victory defined by cowardice hypocrisy. We are polluting our chaste character once held by the highest rank in moral virtue, and if we continue on this path of self ruin and environmental destruction, eventually our fear of mortal vengeance will be the outcome of our future.

CHAPTER 24

WHAT THE HEALTH

I previously exhausted the issue of infinite longevity, and despite that fact I shall continue on this crusade by exploring our devious desperado-like attempt to procuring an unending existence. Basically, I will strive to decipher the pyramid of disarray that is implanted in the vulnerable minds of our receptive population. This form of perplexity is initially provoked by the blatant and obvious contradictions of the notorious medical health reports and statistics. We are a desperate for valuable information society, who have become so entangled in the web of health news, that we will literally alter our entire existence based on these miraculous and revolutionary findings. Thus we gallantly strive forward, living our lives in accordance to these revolutionary findings, only to realize later on that this life saving enlightenment has now become a life threatening alert (due to further and more accurate studies of course). Therefore, I shall escort your impressionable minds through the next few pages, and inevitably I will sacrifice our mismanaged understanding of this medical jargon. The medical world has failed to realize that we hang from their every word, thus this ultimately leads us to victimizing our own personal well being. My ultimate goal is to educate the pilots of medicine. They must come to grips with how much control they have over the mentality of the general population. We have put our lives into your hands, and although I realize that science is far from being exact, you still have an obligation to the world by giving us information that is not going to put our lives in jeopardy. If you have made a miraculous discovery then you must make sure that it has been properly tested and utilized for a great period of time before you volunteer the world as your test dummies (Prisoner experimentation theory remember). You have gained our confidence through your heroic findings, but ironically enough you are losing our trust through reiterated gainsay and recalls.

I must commence this topic with very simple rhetoric by ensuing on a lengthy journey that will ultimately lead us to the truth in health. I will not appoint myself as one who is educated in the medical field, which will leave no chance for my conclusions to be mistaken as remedial advice. The only stake I claim is that of a curious inhabitant on this forsaken planet, who is attempting to find a path led by a survival fitness expert. This search also calls for a non-contradictory guarantee towards a healthy living. Realizing that this fantasy is quite contrary to the accuracy of present day medical reality, I will simply settle for a few definite answers that don't prove themselves to be blatantly conflicting.

I am very well aware of the foods that are considered by definition to be contaminating to the human body. I am also vaguely familiar with the foods that are presumably essential for one's healthful duration, but as I become further entangled in all of this perverted logic, I soon find myself living with a diet that is branded by an array of confabulated mealtime misconceptions. First the authorities on health food maintain that we should sprint in the opposite direction at the sight of an egg, otherwise known as death. Then the infamous *they* say that we should siphon milk directly from the carton or institutionalize hypodermic injection, because this miraculous substance does the body good. However, as these miraculous discoveries of wonderment become a mere figment of our imaginations, a new and more precise study is then released. This time the once devil-possessed egg is the heaven sent cure all for the human body, and the miracle drug milk is now reported to be equally as harmful as the consumption of turpentine. Next *they* proclaim an astonishing announcement by appealing to the use of moderate wine consumption as a healthy heart booster, yet coincidentally one of their colleagues forewarns that a nightly alcohol toddy may lead to a vast disruption in your sleep pattern. Excuse my obvious seizure on the use of over exaggerating sarcasm, however, in comparison it sounds rather subtle in light of these overly misused and radical health reports. It seems rather venturous to release a general studied report involving our routine bodily health, when in fact we are all bred inheriting very diverse genetic ingredients. Every single cure-all physician, heart-smart report, and flaming statistic seem to contradict the true end result. Although I do concur that science is lost in the realm of abstract while reaching towards exact, we shall all be forced to undertake fasting as a safety net if our lives are continually impinged upon. Thus I have reached a historical decision by ensuing a life style designed to fulfill my own edible desires, while mildly sneering at the presence of risk. Therefore, I can only hope that my mealtime rebellion will escort my being into a chance with longevity. I fear that a fifty-fifty percentile is an equation that I am faced with regardless, therefore, I shall create a planner to suit my cravings versus a strict diet that is being guided by the chauffeurs of medical science. I thank you health profession for your time, but in turn I shall snub you for all of the unnecessary chaos.

Bordering this cause is a rather frightening dilemma that entails the advances and consequences delivered with the consumption of prescription drugs. The most successful application in marketing these drugs is provided through the visual aid of television advertisements. Ironically enough this same form of medical broadcast instigates skepticism that has been generated by an array of catalogued side effects. It seems as though you will have to endure a punishment equivalent to making a deal with the devil in order to cure an ailment that doesn't seem nearly as dreadful in comparison to its aftermath. Allow me the pleasure of enhancing your mind power with an authentic example from this bedeviled predicament. A person with allergies must undergo the tremendous seasonal burden that encompasses a bout with watery eyes, drippy nose, and relentless sneezing during an encounter with their enemy to the senses. However, due to the discoveries in medical science, allergies can be suppressed with the simple swallow of a little pill. However, you are to be forewarned that in exchange you will have to tolerate nosebleeds, nausea, light headed spells, and vertigo. Wow, sign me up for the next five years!

The folks for whom I feel the greatest amount of sympathy are those of you who are attempting to shed your excess luggage. Sprint to your doctor for the cure all, because he has a drug for you. He will guarantee the loss of your weight, while peddling to you a few minor side effects. The symptoms you will encounter simply include: stomach cramps, daily diarrhea, and an oily based discharge when you relinquish a breeze from your derriere. Pardon my overly cynical attitude, but if any kind of substance starts blowing out of my buttocks then I would have to take my chances with exercise and will power.

The true demon of all words has now landed on the pages of this chapter. EXERCISE, YUCK! Aside from the typical treadmill junkies, who actually desires this sweaty, muscle aching, energy consuming ritual anyway? I propose that initiating the motivation to exercise should in itself be considered an aerobic workout of the mind. I am altogether awake to the notion that exercise is a vital key to prolonging your body's health and overall survival, but in light of a routine that settles on the feeling of physical loiter, I would much rather train my thumb to demonstrate remote control mastery. Aside from mountain biking, hiking, and general everyday waking, I have completely sacrificed the idea of routine exercise to the numb portion of my brain. I might partake in the joy of aerobics twice annually, but everyday is way beyond my agenda. I am a fairly thin by genetics person, but according to the so called experts I will have just as much of a chance with longevity as a person who is overweight. This is all in the name of failing to exercise. Well excuse me for being indolent, ingrained in my couch, and far too engrossed in my television set to see if my sweat glands are properly functioning. Guess what, Lords of the health environment, hearty folks aren't the only inhabitants who are barbaric towards fitness, so where is your never-ending study about that?

Time and again I must dwell on the obvious in a desired attempt to enlighten this humbled world. Yet, this topic too shall inevitably collect dust in the archives of the barren. As a possibility of logic and reason in the minds of the medical advisories and the general public, we as a society are looking for medical truth, not in theory, but in practical application that is proven to be beneficial in the tangible sense. We cannot depend on the medical world to solely escort us into a life inspired by longevity, and for that we must find a common motivational ground that unites us with an intimate awareness of the mind, body, and soul. Each person must rely on their own ability to strive ahead. Instead, we are setting forth expectations that would demand results conquered by a field that is working without the support of our assistance. We are independent habitants who must take responsibility for our own personal well being, and the rest shall be left to chance. What a difference a day can make.

CHAPTER 25

INTELLECTUAL DEPRECIATION

By definition, the word intellect is described as the mind's ability to think, reason, and learn. However, we as a society have imposed mental stipulations and age limitations on this politically-correct Webster's definitive. As I sit and ponder the issue of intelligence, my mind's eye begins to focus on society's limited mental boundaries. I must compare this scenario to one's ability to personally enhance or neglect their own intellectual potential, which is based on this universally inherited restriction. The reason I have chosen to travel on this path through the mind is because I am an individual who is attempting to explore her intellect, rather than striving to obtain knowledge of my physical limitations. I am faced with the understanding that my thoughts will appear without merit, and they too shall eventually ooze through the cracks of our domain because of my human assigned age. This theory may at first appeal to the ranks of absurdity, however, as I further analyze this psychological misguidance, I hope to instigate a premise that results in acceptance and brings about change. At the end of this mental revolution I shall unveil to the world how our very own intellectual limitations are continually molding planetary inhibitions. This far reaching discovery will inevitably create the mind's dormancy, thus imposing a vast restriction on an individual's potential, and this could prove to be mind shattering during a time when global desperation is at its peak.

I shall begin with the intention of passing the toddler years of life, and I will forge ahead to the stage of puberty. We as a society do not remain in confidentiality about the vast amount of information that is ingrained in the minds of high school pupils throughout their teenage years. Your mind becomes challenged beyond expectation, yet regardless of your proven genius, all of this forced knowledge is stymied by your youthful state of existence and lack of life experience. How ironic it is to be in the midst of time where you are ripening intellectually, yet all of your knowledge is automatically discounted because of your assigned years. If we as a society are to demand of our youth a high degree of intellectuality, then in turn we cannot cheapen this mental agility by repressing their values, opinions, and integral awareness of life. Our youth may be the creators of a fresh approach, and until we permit their voices to be heard aloud, we shall forever remain in the dark when it comes to discovering what scholarly and intuitive gifts they can provide.

Next on this disordered journey of life, we gallantly strive forward to an era where we are perceived as being partially literate and mildly developed; the age better known as our twenties. The education aspect continues to flourish for most, and the experience of real world life finally begins to embark on our department of wits. During this particular time we are universally acknowledged as the adventurous explorers, thus the boundless world teasingly dangles from the edge of our fingertips. We are standing at the base of the almighty mountain, and our intellect is dominated by the superior authorities of wide-reaching experience. We are literally brimming with valuable information that is yet to be discovered, and ironically enough by the time we are merited an outlet to express our knowledge, the value will have descend into uselessness. Allow us to freely contribute to our world, all of the knowledge we have obtained thus far from our surroundings; the universe cannot afford to wait for what society deems as the appropriate age. We are lingering in a time where we can inherit growth from our experiences, but the esteem of our potential is yet again being highly disregarded because of our youth. You must allow us the opportunity to contribute to our world without being sacrificed to this form of rejection.

Following the decade of our twenties, we blossom into the intellectual maturity that accompanies the thirties. Unfortunately during this time in your life you become stalled in a degeneration that permits your ideas in a tangible sense, but denies you merit for your insight. However, on a more enlightening note, you have surpassed the prior obstacles thus allowing you to ascend half way up the mountain top. This grand adventure will allow you to eclipse the former years, and you can now foresee the light of the future. Although true acknowledgment of this time is presented with minimal accreditation, you have gallantly transcended beyond the mere suffocation of your youth. You shall now graduate on to the next fresh and innovative phase of your life. You are enchanted by your mentors in a climb to the highest peak, and propelled by your youthful experiences. The lessons from the prior years have simply transformed into miraculous stepping stones which will bring you closer each day to self discovery and intellectual climax. You are between two eras in time, and your greatest climb in life is only a few stepping stones away.

As we reach the top of the mountain, the fight of forever climbing has at last been conquered. You shall soar into your forties and fifties while transmitting vibes of superior intellect of the mind, body, and soul. As you gaze down on the rest of the world, all shall acknowledge your presence with a bit of admiration and envy. You are now composed of a balanced package that consists of an equal amount of experience and intellect. To mentor the young and elderly is a mission that has become an expectation in the eyes of those who idolize you, and throughout this decade you must escort our society on an enlightening journey into the future. We seek your expertise on life, thus we shall hang from your experience. You shall guide us to the peak of this gigantic mountain so that all shall capture a glance of the superior image that presents itself as the ultimate triumph. To claim victory from the challenge of life is by far the most celebrated experience you shall ever embrace.

Finally, beyond the peak of this mountain lies the valley of immanent wisdom, however, due to your exhausted years the world in your hands has become ingrained as a figment of your imagination. You have surpassed your fifties, and the world surrounding you begins digging your grave. Although you have literally held the world in your hands, your mind has lapsed into a weakening state according to the expectations of a relentless society. Your body and mind may not be able to support the strength in your soul, and so your wisdom becomes a depreciated stigma; affixed to an elderly presence. The world shall cradle you as if your mind has become an intellectual wasteland, and the prior exemplary years are now disregarded and deemed insignificant. Though we as a society have no business robbing you of your intellect and life experiences, we righteously stand by in order to declare you feeble minded. Only you as a human being can decide when your body and mind can sustain you no longer, so you as an individual must remain the authentic mentors of our day and age.

We deem all issues that are generally open to neglect as being insignificant, because we dare not risk the chance for improvement through self evaluation and personal transformation. We are denying one another the ability to intellectually soar, simply because we are following a strict intellectual guideline based on our fallible age agenda. We have formulated a triangular system for our credibility in thinking, and this technique has become outdated in comparison to our valuable potential. Once you have reached your intellectual peak you are virtually praised, however, during your climb to this mountaintop, the rest of your existence is continually plagued by criticism. We have to worship our minds, thus they are vital instruments for our intimate, subjective, and tangible education. This is a mission statement that must be implemented regardless of our age. We must not allow one another to impose limitations on our ability to think and express these thoughts. The mind is a powerful tool, and each individual must represent on their own behalf how to enhance their being through mental acceleration.

CHAPTER 26

LIAR, LIAR, PANTS ON FIRE

During this next chronicle that continues to document the character flaws developed by all human species, I shall dwell on an inherited plague that is ironically hissed upon through a two-faced round of applause. This plight that I must speak of is better known as the little white lie, and I shall assist each of my paragraphs with indisputable examples that acquit our consciences throughout this routine existence byname survival. First I shall meddle through your devious minds in an attempt to unmask all of the lies that children are continually fed by their forefathers during the nurturing developmental years. Parents lie to their offspring in a feeble attempt to fascinate their vulnerable imaginations. Irony is the basis for which each instance ripens, simply because the young are in turn reprimanded for an act that was naively handed down by their predecessor. Next I will journey into the tangled mesh of human interaction, where lying has become a survival skill prerequisite in a culture that has elected authentic truthfulness as an opponent of our day and age. As each passing day inevitably cradles itself into the arms of night, we must continue to fester in the realm of guilt, only to graduate onto the next phase. Whether the words of mistrust are spoken to an acquaintance or a perfect stranger, we are all fouled by this cultural misdemeanor in an attempt to relieve a discomforting situation. Last but not least, I must convey a rather dissimilar scenario that involves humoring an individual's comedic attempt during an occasion that would normally file itself in the category of stale jokes. During a ritual conversation one insists on minimizing their ego for the sake of catering to the likes of those who are vaguely laughable. This form of pseudo-reverence is a rank performance that is enacted simply to pamper the feelings of this self invented comedian. I am truly baffled by the hypocrisy that is gnawing at our moral virtue, and the true conflict arises from our raw denial as creators of this mishap. We as a universal society have mastered the art of lying, and we have devalued our standards in a mouth to mouth cock fight that rewards personal gain amongst a community of followers.

Our parents are the radical professors of the little white lie, and they are contradictors of reprimand when the lie is presented back to them in a divergent situation. When children are vulnerable they are fooled to believe in imaginary characters that deliver to them foil wrapped presents in exchange for cookies. We equally acquaint them with magical fairies who furnish them with money for their homeless teeth. We are constantly preached to about the sin of untruth, yet this contradiction conflicts with a form of lying that is forever implanted in our imaginations. This sense of confusion is rather frustrating to a young mind, because it then becomes quite befuddling when the tiny tots are punished for an act that was ingrained into their perception of right and wrong by their mentors. It is quite unrealistic to spank a child for a lesson learning event that is meant to teach a hands off approach for resolution, and you certainly don't appeal to their quiet side by exercising a voluminous tone if the conclusion is supposed to entail a lesson of mild communication adaptability. Therefore, my perception of parenting is that morals are being corrupted by words of deceit, especially if one is not leading by example. I am fully aware of the fact that my younger years might have been rather dull had I not been given the opportunity to explore my imagination, but in the same breath are we not banking on a system that fully involves unscrupulous hypocrisy? We are inviting into children's minds immoral behavior by teaching them to lie, yet as adults we all know the difference between an acceptable untruth and an act of deception. However, in such an instance the children are unable to fully grasp this concept as it is beyond their years, and by the time they do unravel this bewildering game they may already be scarred by the agony of truth. This is a technique that we are openly supporting, and an embarrassment to our children from which they ultimately suffer.

When an individual adapts to their perception the word acquaintance, they often interpret this being, as a person to whom they have befriended on a more social level, avoiding all sense of intimacy. In exchange for a bout with the close comfort, these familiar faces are more vulnerable to having a brief encounter with the little white lie during a pointless conversation that concludes with the infamous tiding "I'll call you" or "Let's have lunch". In the face of stone cold reality neither party has departed with honorable intention, and the false statement was a radical way to remove one's self from a discomforting situation. We as a society have adapted to a social inconvenience that has bargained with deceit, only to create a warm and fuzzy atmosphere for the moment. Rather than dealing each other a hand of logical honesty, we all assume the role of manipulating players in a game of twisted mind coheres. Instead of ambiguously misleading each other down a dead end path of empty promises, maybe we could inherit a simple departure without fallacious expectations. My point, simply say adios and farewell.

We have also chosen to communicate through a series of misspoken truths, from the bogus cackling of a lame joke, to an entourage of distorted compliments that may pamper one's ego. This is a highly overrated and sensitive instinct where the counterpart chooses to lie in order to spare the feelings of the genuinely needy. A person who is insecure (mind you, this description qualifies the entire human population), will seek out approval from others in order to boost their self esteem for a temporary fix. We are all guilty of promoting deceptive flattery, because the truth shall not free us from the devastating despair that would be inflicted upon the individual in question. In a dissimilar instance, a person's perception of what is witty is again each to their own, but to the time-honored spectator a simple ha-ha may relieve the convictions of this spotlight comic standing before you. Ironically, laughing will only encourage the victim of idle humor, whereas truth of the matter may convince them to scurry along. Thus there are many situations where we must delude the moment with an obvious falsity in order to bolster one's self-assurance, and shall we one day embrace callous honesty we may find ourselves in the clutches of therapy. The harsh reality is one we choose to avoid.

We are in a universal maze amongst lying fanatics, and we perpetually overindulge our egos with double-dealing adulation. Lying has become a native skill that is employed in our everyday existence, and without this masked form of truth we could not survive with confidence. We are relying on each individual for the feel good illusions, which in reality, depict the true weakness imbedded in our cultural core. Should we all initially exist in the realm of truth, then honesty wouldn't have to present itself as the insensitive demon. We are a people conditioned by lies, and for this we shall remain forever with a conscience suspended by fiction. Our existence is guided by deceit, and we follow this path throughout its duration, from the cycle of neonate and beyond forever. If our lives were shaped by truth, then lying would be the error of our ways, but we have chosen the opposite route to travel, and the misguided road to embrace.

CHAPTER 27

THE SHOWER IMPAIRED

I am once again being forced to batter the idea of politeness during this chapter, only because I have been pushed over the suicidal edge of sanity by a growing percentage of the population. Siamese skunks pale in comparison to the stench that accompanies people who refuse to practice good hygiene, and I feel that it is time for someone to step in and make these folks aware of their retched fume. I will not accept poverty as an excuse for filth of the personal being, especially when my worst encounters with smell have been unveiled at my place of employment - a video store. I refuse to apologize for my callus tone and brutal honesty because I along with many others are forced to inhale this fog of rotten stench on a regular basis. I shall approach this issue by declaring war on entire families of inherited stench, then I will bombard the single individual who's smell ranks somewhere in the area of feces. I will conclude this segment by explaining how the rights of society have been infringed on in such a way that we are continually having to inhale the stale aroma of decaying air by those who are foreign to soap. If a cesspool smells like potpourri in comparison to the pollution that is being emitted into the air by the award winners of foulness, then it is time to remove yourselves from the depths of denial, and simply take a damn shower.

I have sacrificed many working years to the business of customer relations, and to this very day I am entirely baffled by a consumer who can squander their funds on frivolous commodities, yet they are completely oblivious towards the fundamentals of using soap. I refuse to believe that an entire family consumed by filth and putrid odor cannot detect through the use of sense how decomposed their neighboring relative reeks. Through the wondrous eye of jaw dropping amazement, this wretched clan has become immune to the odor that defines their silhouette. The polluted steam rolling off of their bodies is deemed normal for those who have tabooed the shower. These are the creatures of human waste who will slink into an establishment five days per week, as they sport around the exact same, grease-speckled outfits. Thus, at the end of the week, the dirties are now sporting around a new and unimproved identity. For instance, the hair is literally sculpting itself, and if grime could be formulated, bottled, referred to as sculpting gel, and fancied with a pristine name, these folks would become multimillionaires. The children have also become so filthy that their gender identity has become in question, however, their fingerprints have now become part of the store décor just incase they do need to be identified. Many folks will riot at my intrusion on their personal state of existence and claim it is an invasion of privacy, but where do my rights exist when the hair on my head begins to part in an attempt to flee from the rancid stench. For example, when a rottenness family walks into a video store with the intention of leaving with nineteen videos and twelve porns (which by the way could make the skin on a potato crawl), then I should be granted the authority to arm myself with a very large can of aerosol air freshener and a butane lighter. I am exhausted by the urgent feeling to vomit on a regular basis, and as simple as the resolution may be, these cretins don't have enough intellect to surface at a department store and buy a bar of generic soap. Of course by the time they bless the world with a bath, the sewage system may back up due to a giant dirt clog. Next the smut household attempts to fulfill the monthly bath quota, but in order to do so they must first fetch after their children in a ritual game of nature's hide-n-seek. Guess what, they're in the backyard camouflaged by the dirt. Point in case, if you want to rot, then fester around in your garbage-filled home, but don't enter the public's domain and suffocate clean society with your stink cloud.

As immunity has now replaced the feeling of utter shock, I am unpleased to announce that the potency of a single individual can out rank that of an entire family. The formal wear of this simpleton consists of an off white tee-shirt, flattered by an array of morning breakfast stains. Sun-baked feces would receive an invitation to a rotting dumpsite before this soiled pedestrian would. Ironically enough, the feces would win by default simply because this decomposing human has a severe breath disease that imitates that of a homeless garlic connoisseur. I have literally encountered mouth air that was so foul, I may very well have conquered the Genus world record for the longest breath ever held by a single human being. Hey, I could hold my breath for a whole week if it means not having to ingest a whiff of air that recently exited a diseased mouth. Many recent amateurs have passed along the advice of breathing through my mouth in order to avoid compromising my sense of smell. Although that strikes me as being a splendid endeavor, the advisement is plagued by many holes. For example, I could politely stand at the service counter with my jaw gaping wide open and resting on the counter, however, I fear that my teeth would rip from my gums and suicide themselves in my stomach acid in an attempt to evade the wretched smell. Aside from the steaming mouth fog, this cretin proudly struts around in a pair of poo-poo stained britches and a fine looking duo of thirty year old sneakers that were possibly coughed up by a giant, garbage siphoning, alley cat. Pardon my harsh critique and judgement upon others, but when a collector of filth forces his stench on my senses, I feel left with no other choice than to declare myself as the potty pants police of the year. Hey, I flutter around the shower on a regular basis, so we should all be required to privilege society with the aroma of clean air. Pollution emerges in many forms, thus society should become part of the solution instead of feeding into the problem.

Lawsuits are becoming frivolous in this society, therefore, I propose that we, the conformists of tidy, form our own government and declare war on the soap impoverished. We will invade the environmental department, and then we will file a nationwide lawsuit against those who have chosen to discriminate against their shower and those who deny themselves the practical application of a toothbrush. I have chosen to apply my skills in a field that involves working with the public, and for that I should not be tortured by the stink of a human who has obviously passed their odor expiration date. If I came into work as a representative of utter filth, then I would literally be ostracized by the entire customer community. Well, hey folks, I am equally disgruntled by a patron who has the buying power of a top notch executive, yet they don't have the funds for a measly bar of soap and a tube of toothpaste. I am a citizen of this country, and alongside countless others, I am demanding a moderately clean consumer. I am not confronting the masters of dirty with unattainable expectations. Instead, I am utilizing the power of suggestion in hopes of hypnotizing those in need. One day they shall find a path to their bathrooms and implement the utilities within. Remember boys and girls, personal hygiene is not a right, it's a necessity!

CHAPTER 28

THE UNIVERSAL STAIN

Seeking out delusional fantasy from television entertainment has become the innovative challenge for a society that takes pleasure from the misery of others. Basically, the general population is addicted to their television sets during times when their own personal endeavors appeal to the side of overwhelming desperation. If one can witness the self-destructive journey another has chosen to travel, then their own personal distress will seem cloudless in comparison. During this particular chapter, I will be probing into the lives of a variety of inhabitants who desire to share with the world their erotic lifestyles and dirty laundry. I shall also touch on the mystery behind the creatures of existence who have literally become obsessively intrigued by human ruination, and how ironic circumstance is presented when another can seem less distressed while focusing on blatant ignorance. Our curiosity has become rather barbaric in that we will attentively sit in wonderment during the airing of a smut Talk Show. Apparently we as a society have become so engrossed in self promotion that we will sacrifice pride in order to capture that moment of fame. People will chatter about anything from prostituted adultery to a consensual triangle sexcapade, and we as the twisted viewer will tune in routinely in an effort to entertain ourselves. After I take you on a magical chauffeur ride into human disgrace, I will introduce the thirty second therapist who enacts the role of drama queen at the tail end of each show. This particular individual has a couple of very limited purposes which include: promoting their own self declared supreme profession and exploiting it as an excuse to escalate the humiliation of those who just spent the last hour justifying their own scandalous actions. Finally I would like to address the issue of politics and the involvement of those who are deciding what a viewer does and does not have the right to watch in the privacy of their own home.

The history pages of our generation will undoubtedly entail the reckless sexual behavior staged during daytime television airspace. The crudest of these particular shows involve a threesome of close friends who at first appear to be tolerable beings, however, they eventually surface as secret sacrificing whores. These harlots eventually volunteer their unsuspecting companion as the unknowing victim of nationally viewed belittlement. The audience is packed with spectators who cheer aloud as one party degrades them at the center of humiliation in an attempt to embrace the almighty spotlight. Thus, they are openly sacrificing any means of dignity while using television as their platform. However, what these attention junkies fail to realize is that they are branding their playboy image on the minds of all who bear a spine, and this foolhardy behavior has deemed them unfit for a majority of the available population. Most of these swindler types will doggy paddle around in their own feces long enough to become noticed by the public, but eventually they will recycle into the depths of yesterday, just before suffocating in their own oxygen wasting carcasses. As for the second cheating guest, they will simply slither back into their snakeskin long enough to prey upon another unlikely couple. The unfortunate victim of circumstance will most likely relinquish any bit of spine they bear for the sake of manipulative amour, unless of course the thirty second televised therapy session can convince the individual to gain enough esteem to flatter themselves with a life change. At the end of each hour, we as the leaches of wretchedness have relinquished our scruples all in the name of personal gain, and we feel relieved to know that our lives aren't nearly as deteriorated as those whom we have recently witnessed.

Allow me to seize the moment for a bit of psychological heckling, and free myself of this therapeutic burden that is yanking on my list of pet peeves. I personally deem it rather useless to appoint an individual as a remedial super hero, who solely depends on and formally swears by a fictitious cure-all. I shall not fail to mention that this miracle approach to speedy therapy is highly overindulged with elevated expectations that are intended to resolve monumental issues before the next commercial break. I am sure the world presents to you a round of applause for your inspirational words of wisdom, but realistically your presence is meant to consume excess air time, and to gouge out the eyes on this panel of nymphomaniacs. However, your effort appears ridiculous when it is shadowed by a destructive collage of unethical engagements brought on by a ruthless gigolo. Although the guidance of virtue that you will assign to each individual guest may prove to be quite valuable, it is unlikely to influence a demeanor that has been subjected to a lifetime of haphazard morals. I bow to the fact that you present to the visitants a bout with hometown counseling, but without the live telecast it is absurd to inherit the concept that these creatures of reckless behavior will give your generosity a second glance. When people volunteer to expose their most intimate sexual demons in view of an entire nation, then the problem is imbedded in their psyche far beyond the calling of a quick fix solution. The therapy segments on these talk shows are being delivered as equally preposterous as the topics themselves. Therefore, the masters of advice should step down allowing for an entire episode of humanity's finest to expose the productivity of their existence. Thus, we as the viewer can awake each morning with the knowledge that there are people out there who have lives that rank more pitiful than our very own.

Next I would like to spew a bit of useless nonsense and declare that politics in comparison to smutty talk shows are, by coincidence, one and the same. We as the viewer have every right to clutter our thought space with useless television garbage, and the ability to do so should not be interfered with by the local government bodies and the anti crusaders. If I want to witness the wrath of some furious housewife, who shall pound the snot out of her life long companion for secretly humping a cousin, then I should be given the opportunity to decide for myself whether or not it is appropriate viewing. Guess what folks, that magical little controller that electrifies your television box with a great source of power, has many other options which include terminating that same mysterious magnetism as well. Besides, if these backwoods, ethical impotent, waste of space junkies, are unscrupulous enough to divulge their sexually impulsive needs or other ridiculous acts on national television, then we as the viewer should behold the power to observe if we choose. I am supposed to rule what is deemed acceptable viewing in my adult only household, and not one single person should be granted the authority to filter my rights. Of course I am speaking within reason, so let's not all jump on the holy roller bandwagon and strike upon me the force of evil. Television is being scrutinized beyond reason, thus we as the audience are all inevitably penalized by a handful of hypocrites that are simply out to make a radical statement through the use of high power and media strangulation. Until we as the people live in pure virtue, and politicians build a platform unsupported by closet skeletons, then don't present to me what is deemed a moral course of proper action.

Realistically our lives could exist fruitfully without the presence of talk shows, however, since they already reside as a part of our lives, the issue still remains. Many shows have proven to be informative in an acceptable manner according to the standards we pose to live by. However, ironically enough, the highest rated shows have proven to be those which have no standards at all. This in turn questions our vow to righteousness and simply proves that we exist as immoral closet junkies. Most of these smut shows do not have to search the world over to find the dirty laundry, thus the trash is usually lingering right outside their doors. Yes, I too am baffled by the vast fleecing of immoral America, but until we collaborate as a whole to make the world a peace-loving Woodstock, then we really don't stand a chance against the calamity of our dismay. Hey, as long as there is a person willing to exchange pride for fame, then there will always be a listener with their ear pressed against the glass. Talk shows are by far not the only programs that openly exploit scandalous acts created by human inferiority, they are simply a coalition of mockery that gained a vast amount of generated popularity. Until we as the people transform our standard of living, and change how we present this ritual animation, then realistically we only have ourselves to blame. It is easy to condemn television as the source of the world's sinful wrong doing, but the true difficulty is to acknowledge where the problems actually begin. Until we take responsibility for this dishonor to our culture, then we shall never open our minds to the wisdom that enlightens change.

CHAPTER 29

THE HUMANE SACRIFICE

During the near closing of my discourse on humanity, I shall escort our emotions on a dismal and dreary psychotic tour of the anti-humans who stalk their prey. We as the formally untainted might better be recognized to these behemoths as an imminent casualty. This particular blackened chauffeur ride will involve an indirect confrontation with a specific coalition of menacing felons, and I must attempt to debilitate their self justified ability to commit heinous acts on their own kind. First I will encounter the demons who forcefully rape the unsuspecting, and I must sink deeper into their pitch black aura for the ultimate satisfaction of exploiting their distorted logic. Next I will sacrifice all armed robbers, feeding them to the wolf-like instincts of the terror-stricken. Through the irony of fate they shall suffer at the hands of torment that will escalate from a barrage of carefully selected sentence fragments. Finally, I would like nothing more than to immerse my thought process into the venomous transgressors, and emerge with the self determined insight that manipulates the mind of the bloodthirsty slayer. To spawn into a manmade Satan with the intent of eliminating life, is by far the most horrific display of human work that shall ever accompany us in this twisted game of survival. A surreal fated reality may embody these pages equivalent to that of a hypothermic fury, and those with natural emotion will experience an arctic chill that shall breathe upon the fringe of your weary spines. Criminal repulsion ranges with circumstance, thus the number far outweighs my ability to exploit them all. However, as an individual who exists on the grounds of this planet, I am exhausted by the need to forever protect my personal being from the mentally crazed and the carnal assault inflicted by another. This implanted fear in my mind is dictated by the knowingness that someday I could become the victim of a violent crime. We can continue to exist as a species that is ruled by this inferno of hatred, or we can unite as a whole and regain control of our glorious kingdom. A person who fights for a cause has only their pride to gain, but an entire collection of people that work together can instigate a premise that demands a result brought on by change.

You stalk our world withholding all regret that accompanies the essence of remorse, thus your darkened core shall siphon the spirit of another from the depths of their soul. To prey upon a defenseless victim instigates an artificial emotion that you will forever be denied, and this form of spiritual emptiness has fueled a tempered fury that boils within your callused veins. A bitter manifestation towards the polar gender, who attempted to escape your wrath, has become the driving force for which you justify an implacably sexual ravishing. Your demon within will eternally prosper at the hands of injustice for a crime that you will never internally be held accountable for, and your victim, who will forever suffer with an emotional scar, is simply another being toward whom you inflict pain without compassion. Life has offered to you a series of choices that you bartered away for the sake of sexual desperation. The struggling of the weak is burned on your photographed memories, and everyday cradles an intense despair that emerges into a distorted game of this sexually deranged hunt. This world sustains you as a being, and when the humane are lost to a freak coincidence, I choose to question what force would allow for such ill mercy. How you came to thrive on such a vehement demeanor, is by far the reality to which we as a culture may eternally remain oblivious. During a time in your own existence you must have encountered the face of constrained evil, and now you have selected to portray your own misfortune of circumstance on the unsuspecting. The retched wickedness that rules your life will eventually become sacrificial, and when death strikes, thus ripping your soul from your being, eternity may sanction you to the bloodcurdling depths of all unfeasible horror.

Surrounded by the feeling of comfort and stability in the privacy of your home or work environment is an image that is being destroyed with the passing of each day. When the occasion is least expected, a psychotic mind, ruled by violent greed, will force upon you a frenzy that devours the warmth of your life-long security blanket. This type of mentally volatile creature will instill a vast amount of fear in their victim, yet their own cowardly state of existence is ironically strengthened through the threat of a dangerous weapon. This form of desperation that stimulates poison in their psyche is presumably generated from the adrenaline elevation during an armed robbery. This creature will seize valuable possessions, and they will perform this act at the secured end of a weapon. Aside from violently purloining valuables, these public monstrosities will pillage the pride and esteem from another, which in turn momentarily satisfies their own internal deficiencies. Focusing on items of value will surely suffocate the worthless, drug induced existence, that one who enforces violence is burdened to live with. These creatures are either poverty stricken, or they simply bear a ruined conscience, and they will terminate a life if their plan to wealth is interfered with. The truth of the matter is that any creature who has captured the idea of wealth through any means of severity has made a fated deal with the red horned diabolic, and their everafter is lost to the realm of hellfire eternity without exoneration. Always keep in your reserve that in a moment least expected, there will not be a shield to protect you from the wrath of your own bullet.

When one appeals to the concept that the human species couldn't possibly be any more vulgar, there is yet another being that will fit the mold of horrific, insane, and demented. This type of antichrist symbolizes the foundation of all vicious evil, thus they will perpetually survive feeding off of their own possessed reality. Senseless murder is by far the most heinous brutality one individual could enact upon another, and these wretched murderers will forever seethe throughout eternity without feeling the least bit of remorse for their victims. It is a horrific display of ignorance that we as emotionally encompassing human beings would allow the survival of a black and tainted soul. We pamper them, we feed them, and we give them a peaceful night's sleep, and in the end, the victim's memory and rights are lost to a cradling justice system. The weakest of all mankind is disguised by the treachery of their own actions, and those who must capture the last breath of air from a living creature are impurely soaked with the devils blood. Whether the occurrence is delivered in this lifetime or beyond, punishment is inevitable, and one shall not escape from the depths of its merciless wrath.

Our once-upon-a-time primitive castle is now swelling with an extremely desensitized version of humanity. Instead of catering to these demoralized human beings, we should be enforcing severe penalties that would serve as a sure fire preventative. If a rapist was sentenced to a mandatory removal of his genitals after forcefully violating the innocent, then I guarantee the freely roaming conglomeration of sex offenders would decline into near extinction versus violating their prey. The civil rights clan will undoubtedly lash out in a rage that spews cruel and unusual barbarity against another human being, but when the rights of victims are overshadowed by the rights of a criminal, then we as a society are being self blinded by a failing legal system. Being horrifyingly violated is the definition of inhumane attack, thus the offenders should be terminated of their rights instead of being pampered by them. If we as a society do not implement an effective safeguard against violence, then we will always be conveying an unspoken permission to the entire coalition of venomous assailants.

CHAPTER 30

THE HIGH SCHOOL REUNION

As I exit the reality of this remarkably animated journey, I must declare that this particular adventure, in the realm of the here and now, has been one of my most exhilarating and therapeutic experiences thus far. I am unable to fully relish in my finished effort until I illuminate my magical destiny with one last fascinating topic. Within this glorious awakening I shall welcome my fellow peers to our forthcoming, ten year, class reunion. Before we begin our long winded conversations that detail a catalogue of life success stories and otherwise, we must first honor the majestic experience with a round of applause. This eminent moment must entail a vivid glimpse of life in general, because this miraculous gift is so very precious, and within the depths of our own misguided invincibility it could forever expire without cause. When the opportunity has rejuvenated our souls, we shall continue on with an open minded view of the unique and diverse paths that we have all chosen to walk. Escorted by an essence of pure virtue, the room will fill with a remarkable collection of wonderful memories and intriguing encounters that have guided us since our graduation day. Let us share with each other our experiences in life, whether pleasant or tainted, without being attacked by the wrath of one's egotistical judgement. Thus we have all encountered at least one eye opening hurdle that has truly rekindled the meaning of life and our reason for existing. With confidence I must embrace the theory that we have superseded the stereotypical dilemma that has burdened our youth, and with the closing of one chapter, another shall emerge. Therefore, we can embrace the comfort that cradles a reuniting with a former pal, and liberate our minds with an enlightening perspective that acquaints itself with the invitation of a newfangled companion. Life does not always mold itself into the pattern that we first envisioned, but if you can emerge from each day with a bright minded realization, then the rest will eventually fall into place.

As each day dashes by in a race to the eternal finish line, most of our friends who toured with us through our high school years, will simply become a vague memory or a random acquaintance. Life passes down yet another encounter with irony when the pals we cherished during our youth become virtual strangers. Life is a buoyant journey for which we all choose our own expressway, and for most high school companions it is a destination that draws beyond ourselves and guides us on a path of separation. Through an arranged coincidence our tracks will cross again one day, and from that moment on we can re-ignite a disillusioned flame, or we can continue to walk opposite of our yesteryears. We shared countless gleeful and not so gleeful occasions which will open the gateway of reminiscing, and the following years will create a platform from which we can soar to a higher level of acquaintance. It is quite possible that our once upon a time friendship was a convenience for the moment, but a reunion is our window of opportunity to rediscover what has been lost by chance. For those of you who walked with me through that journey, I will always carry for you a special place within my being. The moments we shared together lie as a silhouette to the person who I have become today. For those of you who made hellfire eternity seem brighter in comparison to the occasions spent with you, I send my sincere regards. Without your endless ridicule throughout a greater part of my school experience, I would never have gained the strength to rise above the misery. Whether good or bad, I thank you all for the times we had.

A decent percentage of our peers chose to embark on the bliss of domestic engagement, thus they have adopted the bonds of premature marriage and overabundant child bearing. I am 25, and I couldn't imagine having a kid even now, and the fact that I killed a cactus and a Chia pet all in the same year, simply reinforces my fear of parenting. However, my impotent nurturing skills have nothing to do with those of you who are probably great parents, so let's move on. Unfortunately, those of you who have become parents will most likely endure a vast amount of degradation from a clan of classmates whose idea of success is limited to a college degree and employment status. However, as the years have quickly faded, many of these same vainglorious colleagues have realized that life is not a detailed itinerary highlighted by a strict timeline. A glorious family life is the route that you have chosen to travel, and you have been instilled by a form of maturity that most will not cherish for years to come. Your children, a pure innocence, are the bearers of your spiritual mind, body, and soul, thus they have become a pure miracle in this natural world. Regret will never burden your existence, if you can hold within your heart that parenting for most is a truly beautiful phenomenon that many folks will forever live without experiencing. You will shape their lifelong journey, and you are the protectors of their internal inclinations. We survive on a mentality that frowns upon your developing lifestyle, but your window to the world is the only view that will remain authentic to your offspring. Therefore, when you walk with an elaborate nonchalance into our long lost reunion, you shall carry yourself with pride, knowing that you have blessed our world with your own little miracles. Unless of course you are one of America's many dysfunctional families, then you may want to start setting aside funds for your child's therapy sessions. Forget college, they'll be too mentally deranged and out of their skull by that point. Congratulations, you're raising the mentally insane.

The most self-indulged and arrogant preoccupation one will obsess on after their post high school existence, is the security of a prominent career. A majority have set lucrative goals that will surely boost their status in this world, but many of these same modern day hustlers will lose their ambitions in the reality of everyday life. A few of you will achieve exactly what you set forth initially to do, and the rest of us may spend an entire lifetime searching for our true calling. When fate reunites our present with our past, a conversation emerges that will fixate on our immediate livelihood, and during this dreadful revelation we shall squirm with indignity until the moment fades. Many will battle for career-acquired bragging rights, while the remainder will stand modestly in an attempt to evade the almighty spotlight. We have not embarked on self discovery, thus a bout with simplicity is the road less traveled. We were set free on this meandering path of life, and while attempting to cross the intertwine, we all experienced the consequence beheld by a wrong turn. If you are the type of individual who simulates a life mirrored by perfection, then you must unveil the truth to your genuine identity. It is acceptable to exist without polished excellence because forging out a path of mistakes to learn from is how one becomes fulfilled by wisdom. Some inhabitants will spend the their entire lives focused on a triumphant career, and if that is what allows them to exist comfortably, I tip my hat to their ambition. However, many of us will be eternally consumed by the search that unmasks our true being, and if we execute this from within the walls of a simple job, that by comparison is just as respectable. It is not the responsibility of others to define one's success, because like beauty, prosperity is in the eye of the beholder. Life is what you make it, so enjoy it for what it is.

Life is a vividly animated voyage, and we as the aimlessly wandering will spend an entire lifetime trying to figure out the mystery behind it. The greatest truth that I have discovered thus far is that you must engage in the experiences that lie true within the depths of your being. This personal endeavor might be found in a gratifying career, the lineage of your soul, or simply a never-ending search for a more fascinating adventure than those you had captured the years before. Along the way we will be beset by a series of obstacles, but possessing the inner strength to conquer these barriers is a lesson in success to which many will forever be blinded. To see beyond the external frame, thus looking at a more picturesque vision, is inevitably where the cloud will meet with its silver lining. May your lives everlastingly carry you beyond all limitations.

≈ **PEACE** ≈

SUMMARY

While I was writing this book, anxiety and self doubt began flooding my mind, thus my hunger for uninhibited expression was nearly destroyed by an overwhelming amount of fear. My style of writing is rather crude and tasteless at times, thus I panicked over the mere thought of being chastised by the majority of society. However, I spent several years withholding my ability to write, and within my reserves idled an extreme need to express. Although I explored many alternatives, I was never able to discover a way that freed my ability to verbalize without caution. I do acknowledge the fact that at times my criticism crossed over the fine line of being outright judgmental, however, a mild form of discrimination is simply an effect of spontaneous writing. I am not some self righteous troll that sits on top of my golden pedestal, thus casting down harsh examinations on those whom I've deemed beneath my level. I am simply a writer who has conveyed to the world an elongated list of learned lessons that spawned from a collection of my own personal mistakes. To consider myself above my fellow man is a reckless frame of mind that would only prove to have disastrous consequences on my search for truth in life. In a theatrical sense, I am merely a fish in a pond that consists of my equals, and from these murky waters I can see clearly now. It is easy to shoot from the hip and hit the target by chance, but if one can step back and observe the territory first, then experience will come without question. Every single issue that I touch on is not a the creation of my fictional mind, I am simply writing about the world as I know it to exist.

Kristina Landers

ABOUT THE AUTHOR

My name is Kristina Landers, and I am 25yrs. of age. Currently I am working as an Assistant Manager in retail, and like many others, I am confined to a mind numbing job that is sucking the life out of my body and soul. However, from my background in existing, and through my career in public relations, I have been able to observe first hand the distinct idiocies of our culture, thus I must release this elongated list of pet peeves from the perpetually agitated part of my thought process. As I state in the Introduction of *The Tainted View,* I am just an average Joe, thus I do not deem myself as being greater, smarter, or any more successful than the average person. I am simply tortured by the idea of taking a backseat to all of the empty-headed cretins on this planet, and I am rightfully taking a stand.

I had been searching for many years to find my place in this world, and finally, through *The Tainted View*, I have discovered my calling in life. Previously I attempted to write a romance novel, however, when I was completed with the book, it was approximately five pages in length. Apparently their isn't a high demand for romance pamphlets in the market, so inevitably it had to be put to rest. You can get to know me on a more intimate level in the Introduction, Text, and Summary of my book. I truly believe that people are endlessly searching for that to which they can personally relate, so this is what I offer to them...

I am confident when I say that every single person alive has been fueled by the ignorant actions of another. Do you remember the last time you felt rabid by the careless driving habits of another? How did you feel the last time an emotionally impotent man spouted out a sarcastic remark about PMS? Were you jumping for joy the last time you stood in line at the supermarket, behind a family with two parents and ten kids, while they proudly paid for an array of brand name food products with food stamps? Hey, I am equally as exhausted by a society that has become too self preoccupied in life that their actions have ignited a race that is rewarded by the demise of intellect and pride. In *The Tainted View*, my topics of discussion range anywhere from, PMS to road rage, all the way to annoying customers, litter junkies, and free loading parasites (stay tuned, there is much much more).This is a tainted journey that will forever implant itself in the pet peeve portion of your mind. *Entertainment purposes only, not to be taken as remedial advice.